PRIMARY WHITES

PRIMARY
WHITES

A NOVEL LOOK
AT RIGHT-WING POLITICS

BY ANONYMOUS
AS TOLD TO CATHY CRIMMINS
AND TOM MAEDER

DOVE
BOOKS

ISBN 0-7871-1104-X

Printed in the United States of America

Dove Books
8955 Beverly Boulevard
West Hollywood, CA 90048

Distributed by Penguin USA

Text design by Stanley S. Drate/Folio Graphics Co., Inc.
Jacket illustration, design, and layout by Rick Penn-Kraus

First Printing: April 1996

10   9   8   7   6   5   4   3   2   1

To the anonymous writers, speechwriters, and spin doctors who make the world go round.

1

My role in the campaign started with a bang. Literally.

I would see him fire a gun many times after that, and I still don't understand just how he does it. He is a large, fleshy man with a broad face, a dimpled chin, and eyes that squint when he smiles. The .357 Magnum was dwarfed in his strong, muscular palm, no doubt developed over all those years of pencil-pushing.

I'm afraid of guns. I was deafened by the noise and heard only half our conversation that day, yet even now I remember it as one of the most important I ever had. Wearing his comical earphones, focused on the target, he still had enough energy to make it seem like all his attention was fixed on me. After all, he was a former speechwriter—he knew how unimportant actual words often are.

His posture, his relaxed stance—in fact, everything about him—made me think of all those Wild West movies I'd seen as a kid. Here was the kind of man, a pioneer, who had settled the open spaces, pushed back the frontiers, and now that we knew the limits of America, here was the kind of man who could help us shut those frontiers down.

In spite of my fascination with the man, I couldn't help but jump every time he fired a shot. Yet he seemed not to notice. Instead, he slapped a pistol into my hand, along with an NRA button. "Are you a straight shooter?" he yelled, grinning.

An attendant shoved some earphones onto my head. I tried my best not to panic. The bull's-eye was barely visible at the far end of the firing range. I took aim, hoped for the best, and squeezed. Nothing happened.

"Lock and load," he said. "You can't shoot without bullets, pilgrim."

I turned red—I color easily—and looked down at my hand, trying to figure out where the bullets were supposed to go. What did "lock and load" mean, anyway? I fumbled stupidly with the weapon.

"I hear you're thinkin' of takin' a shot at the presidency," a sexy female voice behind us said to my companion. It was Jolene Raybuck, curvaceous owner of Satan's Shooting Range. She held up a life-size paper target of President Jeb Clanton. "Why don't you start right now? Pull out that big gun of yours and take a pop!"

Jolene ceremoniously attached the president's effigy to the automatic range line. It was a remarkably good likeness, though a little thinner than he looked in real life. Jolene pushed a button. Faster than you can say "Hail to the Chief," Paper Jeb zipped off down the range.

I braced myself for the explosion, but none came. He took aim, then stopped and put down the gun. He turned and gazed upon the crowd. Then Mike J. Duncannon, candidate for president of the United States, surprised all of us. He began to make a speech.

"Thanks, Jolene. Many Americans would kill for this opportunity. Every right-thinking citizen wants to blow away the last three years of incompetent, liberal, homo-loving, godless government." Duncannon gestured expansively down the range. "And now, there you are, Mr. President. Out there, twisting in the wind. I'm honored to accept the nomination to stand in for millions of voters and show you what America thinks of you and your policies.

"But, as much as I would like to shoot down your sorry political career, I'm going to give somebody else a crack at it."

Duncannon turned to me and gave me his gun: "Here, Harry, take mine."

"Ladies and gentlemen—and children—may I introduce Harry Beltway, grandson of one of the most beloved and important preachers of all time, Mr. Billy Beltway."

The little crowd gathered around us clapped. That was how it began. I honestly thought I was just coming by to shake hands and consider the possibility of working for Mike Duncannon. I didn't expect to shoot the president.

"But he's the Commander-in-Chief," I protested. I sounded like a grade-school kid.

"Awww, he's just a man, Harry," Duncannon said impatiently.

I shook my head. "Please, sir—show me how to knock off an incumbent."

He took back his revolver and blazed away. The shooting gallery fell silent as the crowd watched the tattered Jeb Clanton target travel back to the man who was gunning for his spot.

Duncannon had aimed below the belt. He looked at the

pattern of his bullets and smiled. "Well, he's not the man he used to be."

Suddenly a tall woman looking exactly like Duncannon in a dress swept into the room. "Boys, boys, boys—I know you're getting off on this, but don't shoot your whole wad here. Besides, the real Jeb Clanton is a moving target. Mike, did you forget that we've got that speech this afternoon?"

"Awww, Day! Just a few more minutes. You gotta try this, too."

The woman, whom I had immediately placed as Duncannon's cousin and campaign manager, stared back in silence.

"Just a *few more shots*?" Duncannon whined.

"C'mon, Mike, give me a break, okay?"

"Women, Harry. You can't live with 'em—"

"And you can't run a campaign without 'em," continued Day Duncannon. "You must be Harry Beltway. Mikey and I grew up listening to your grandfather's sermons."

"Yep, in our Catholic neighborhood, they said that when the pope needed advice, he called Billy Beltway," said her cousin.

I chuckled nervously. I was never comfortable when people brought up the subject of my grandfather, the old hypocrite. If they only knew what had gone on under those robes. "Well, there were people who thought my grandfather was more Catholic than the pope back then. Pope John, right?"

"That's right, the liberal one," said Day, turning all businesslike again. "Let's go, guys. Jolene—thanks for everything."

"Yeah, it's always a pleasure to drop by. You have a really nice place here, Jolene, but you ought to get yourself a nice fence," Mike added.

We got into the Lincoln stretch limo.

"Lincoln, the first Republican president, and a great car," said Duncannon. (I would hear this joke at least nine hundred times in the next six months.) He switched on the small color television, reached into the refrigerator for a beer, and lunged for the cellular phone.

"Mike—the phone bill!" said Day, who was already settling in to watch Marcia Clark talk about blood, gloves, and white Broncos. "I like her suit," she muttered.

"Yeah, honey, a little shooting," said Duncannon into the phone. "It was cute. They brought out a Jeb Clanton target. Shoot the prez—just call me Lee Harvey Duncannon. . . . Un-huh. Yeah . . . Day and I are riding with Harry Beltway—you knew his grandfather, back when we worked for Dick. . . . Un-huh. So we're riding together, trying to get Harry to help us out. And we're getting our O.J. for the morning, too. God bless CourtTV. . . . Yeah. I know. What a waste of our judicial system. All that money. I could call my friend Darryl Dent—he knows a cheaper way to get rid of uppity *African Americans*."

"Honestly, Mike," groaned Day. Then she laughed wickedly. "You know the trees aren't sturdy enough in California for that sort of thing. They're just gonna have to nail the Juice *legally*. Time is money," she added, tapping her watch and pointing to his cellular phone.

"Honey, I gotta go. But I wanted to call to tell you I'm bringing Harry to dinner. . . . So can you call and add one to the reservation? Yeah. . . . Me too. Bye now."

Duncannon set down the phone and smiled at me. "My better half. I'm a lucky man—two great gals to take care of me. Day takes care of me from the neck up, and then there's Sherry. She's responsible for the belly.

"Now, Harry, what can you do for me?"

A good question. The call from Duncannon's office had been a surprise: I'd only been back in the country for a few weeks. Sure, I had made the rounds to see my college friends on the Hill, but the conversations had all seemed casual, exploratory. Living in Africa for the last two years definitely had not prepared me for the jungle drums of Washington. Within days, even hours, everyone knew I was back. And, in their infinite wisdom, the right-wing powers that be attempted to suck me back into the system.

Back in '92 I worked for Jody Braggart, a philandering evangelist I now refer to as Judas, who hankered after the presidency. He was a major disappointment. His manic-depressive notion of redemption upset me so much, it was hard to get up each morning to make the phone calls. I began to feel out of touch with mainstream politics. I might as well have been working for a Martian or a lesbian nun.

Last night Sam Magillicuddy, Duncannon's assistant campaign manager, had left a message where I was staying, at the YMCA in downtown D.C., that Duncannon wanted to see me. By morning, a taxi voucher was waiting for me at the front desk along with the address of the shooting range.

Maybe I shouldn't have been *that* astonished to be pressed into service. Few fellows can claim to be as much of an aristocrat of the religious right as myself—a Beltway, of *the* Beltway Jesus superstars, a whole family of savvy evangelists who turned praising the Lord into a cottage industry. Even the fact that I was the son of the family's only black sheep didn't seem to bother people when they were looking to add cachet to their staff. My father, Tobias, had been the child superstar of the Beltway Family Preachers until he pulled a Marjoe Gortner and freaked out at the age of eighteen. Suddenly he realized there was a whole wide world out there, and he wanted to be part of it. He was luckier than Marjoe, though—his parents let him live out his rebellion, sending him to Middlebury College and then on to Yale Drama School, where he majored in Brechtian acting. Billy Beltway was wise enough to cut his losses early, give Dad a sizable sum, and hope that he would disappear. And he did. He married a wealthy bohemian girl, Kelly Huntingdon, and moved to the south of France, where they started an avant-garde puppet theater and gave birth to me, an evangelistic throwback. Somehow the love of Jesus had skipped a generation, and my parents recognized it almost immediately. Every summer they sent me back to North Carolina, where I frolicked with my many cousins amid the revival tents and church socials.

And so I fell, rather effortlessly, into the role of junior evangelist. My trips back to France became fewer after my grandparents enrolled me in military school, and my mother's topless sunbathing and Dad's godless artist friends began to embarrass me. They still do. Not that there weren't a few worms in my new Eden's apple. Let's just say that Billy Beltway and his colleagues disappointed me on many occasions, and did so with more hypocritical zeal than my poor, misguided parents could ever muster. Mom and Dad were harmless.

They're both back in the States now, married to different people. Neither of them uses the Beltway name, even though Dad still lives off the pennies raised for Christ.

Mom and Dad could escape—go, if you will, outside the Beltway—but I know now that *I* never can. Even two years in Africa as a missionary didn't cure me of wanting to be a part of Republican politics. Preaching Jesus to Third World losers didn't curtail my ambitious streak. I dreamed of running a campaign for a moral, upstanding guy who wouldn't disappoint me by getting caught in a scandal. I believed in everything that Duncannon stood for. I had long admired his ability to harness others' fanaticism and make it work for him politically. I was ready for a purely conservative experience, maybe even one where I had a chance to win, or at least shine.

Was this my moment? Was Duncannon my window of opportunity? I couldn't wait to find out, but I was still willing to play hard to get for another day, or at least for a few more hours.

Now Duncannon had asked me what I wanted to do for him, and I wasn't sure.

"More to the point, what can I do for *you*?" he said.

"Well, that depends," I said, sitting back and attempting to look blasé. An uncomfortable silence ensued.

"Harry, we need you," said Day, who had switched off the O.J. channel so that she could close in for the kill. "You were wonderful with Jody Braggart—you were the only one who really knew the score. We've been trying to get in touch with you for over a year now, and we're so glad you've finally returned from the Heart of Darkness."

As if on cue, her cousin began an African-style chant: "A-boom-bop-a-boom-bop-a-BOOM!"

"Harry, check us out," continued Day, fixing me with her glacial stare. "We have a shot. We think we have a good chance of changing things that really count. You know, it's one thing to preach to people with no hope at all, like your precious natives. But it's a whole other thing to have the ear of the greatest nation in the world. You'd be bringing good, wholesome values to the people of America."

"Day, enough with the hard sell," said Mike.

"Sometimes I think I'm not ready to spin miracles again," I said. "I wish I could believe that this whole crazy mess could make sense." Then I stared back, even harder, at Day: "Haven't you ever had doubts? I heard you were, um, out of it for a while."

"I was out of the *country*, Harry, not out of my mind, if that's what you mean. You sound like you think I was in the booby hatch or something. I went to Australia back in 1974. I was disgusted, Harry. Watergate did me in. It destroyed my faith in the American system. So I went to Australia because I thought it was like what America used to be—wild and open and free, a country where hard-working folks could still make their fortunes and oppress the indigenous peoples. Of course that's all gone now, too. But I spent a couple of years there. Hunted crocodiles in New Guinea, prospected for opals and gold. Got married. Had a few kids. It made me feel like a new woman. And I became a Mormon, Harry, which is the one good, true, old made-in-the-USA religion with none of this import stuff. It kind of made me feel nostalgic, so then I came

9

back here to America, figuring that if I didn't like it I could change it. And I did, Harry. I signed dollar bills for Donald Degan, and I helped out in Gordon Hedge's campaign, but then I decided the best thing I could do was to get my cousin Mike elected. Our pop always said that we should keep things in the family, that family was everything, and that the Duncannon family was the best. So here we are, Harry. And we're going to win."

"Aw, Day, let the kid breathe," said Duncannon, grabbing a file from his briefcase. "But you should know, Mr. Beltway, this isn't an impulse buy. You come highly recommended."

"Yeah, Harry, you sure do," said Day. "You'd be a great addition to our team. But don't make up your mind yet. Come along with us today for a while. Mike would also like to take you to dinner later, and in a few minutes you'll see what Mike can do to an audience."

And so we rode out to Fairfax, where Duncannon was supposed to give a speech to hundreds of Tupperware employees. He and Day had switched on C-SPAN. I sipped a Diet Coke. After a while Duncannon opened the file on his lap and began to go through his speech. He started whistling.

"Really, Mike. That's annoying," said his cousin.

Duncannon laughed. "But I'm just whistling 'Dixie,' honey. It's a great song, isn't it, Harry? A great protest song, now that I think of it." He pulled a small notebook out of his lapel pocket and jotted something down. " 'We Shall Overcome,' 'Dixie'—they're both great protest songs! Gotta use that, somehow."

Mike Duncannon. Consummate candidate, consummate

speechwriter. I had to admit it fascinated me—he seemed to do it all himself. While others had scores of handlers and writers and image consultants, he was ready to go it alone. He had spent years crafting words for others, all the time, it seems, waiting in the wings for the day he could put words into his own mouth. And now his day had come.

The Tupperware employees went crazy for Mike Duncannon, and so did I.

He came on stage to deafening applause, waited for the silence, and then burped—loudly. "Ah . . . the Tupperware burp. One of the best sounds in America." Great laughter. Then he proceeded to wring incredible metaphorical possibilities from his audience's product.

"But seriously—yours is a great enterprise, a great company in a great country. You sell a great product to people who need it, and you enable women to bring money into the home without abandoning their families. What is it that really liberated American women? Not a gaggle of feminist blowhards, but malls, supermarkets, dishwashers, disposable diapers, frozen foods, and—Tupperware. Without citizens like you, America would fester. Because what is Tupperware, really? It is protection. It is a boundary that locks in freshness and locks out the germs and parasites of the outside world. We need those boundaries, and we need to take back America from the lurking threats that could spoil it forever. And what are we gonna keep in those many-shaped containers that we've worked so hard to make? It sure as hell ain't sushi! (Applause.) It ain't tacos! (More applause.) It ain't Ethiooooopian sponge bread!" (The crowd was now standing on its feet.)

He continued in this vein—or refrigerator compartment, if you will—for a full twenty minutes, giving them a tailor-made stump speech that made them feel extruded plastic containers were the last bastion of freedom in the Western world. Afterward, dozens of middle-aged ladies pressed upon him stacks of aqua and hot-pink plastic boxes filled with caramel popcorn and chocolate chip cookies and bread and butter pickles. Most he handed over to the Tupperware officials, but he kept a few for the ride back. Day, who seemed very pleased at the way the speech had gone, rolled her eyes as her cousin started wolfing down some black-and-white brownies.

"You'll lose your appetite for dinner at your fancy Jockey Itch Club," she said.

The Jockey Club at the Ritz-Carlton is one of those places that looks frozen in time—1963, to be exact. Cultural diversity has not made any inroads there, and the place has happily escaped all major trends of the past three decades, including exposed brick, chintz, sponge-painted walls, and waiters who want to establish an intimate relationship with their hapless customers. If guys had wombs, they would probably be paneled, filled with red leather couches, and lined with steaks, just like the Jockey Club. I felt comfortable the moment I walked in—it reminded me of all the clubby restaurants I had gone to over the years with my grandfather.

"Order an appetizer, too, Harry. Are you a steak man?" asked Duncannon. I had found him alone at a table in the front room, holding court as lobbyists and Hill celebrities passed by. He had seemed relaxed earlier in the day, but now his posture suggested total comfort. He was like a lizard who had found his perfect microclimate.

"Ben McCord!" he trumpeted. "Get your butt over here!" McCord was the popular conservative host who had given Duncannon his start as the video pin-up boy of the Right. McCord was surrounded by an entourage of earnest young guys in tortoiseshell glasses—probably the staff of his TV show. He hurried by, taking Duncannon's hand and squeezing it in transit. "I'm late, Mike," he said. "Whaddya think of that piece about you in *The New Republic*? Listen, call me soon. Try the tuna carpaccio. It's great tonight."

"The girls are in the Ladies'," Duncannon said as he watched Ben McCord sweep out. He motioned the waiter to fill my glass with some of the Kistler Chardonnay from the wine bucket at his side. He must have thought I glanced disapprovingly at the bottle's California label. "I used to prefer a nice Pouilly Fuissé," he said, "but I try to drink American now." He lifted his glass. "Here's to America! So whaddya think? Am I a contender?"

"Sir, you're a wonderful speaker. I think you would make a great candidate."

"And you—what do you want from life, now that you're Out of Africa?"

"Well, I'm considering my possibilities."

"Consider this one."

I felt two tiny hands clasp my shoulders from behind. I started and turned around to face the Perfect Political Wife. About forty-five, forty-six. Pretty. Highlighted bronze hair in a tasteful flip, frosty pink nails, and Pendleton wool blazer. That imperturbable Kabuki-like mask that registers constant faux delight.

"Harry, I would like you to meet my wife, Sherry."

"The famous grandson of a man who touched all our lives. How do you do? Mike has told me so much about you." She daintily took a seat next to Duncannon. He beamed. Day stood looming over the table looking like Sherry's goofy teenaged daughter.

"Gotta go. Gotta see the boys," said Day.

"I really wish you would stay," said Sherry sweetly.

"Oh, Day doesn't approve of expense account dining," said Duncannon. "Let her go home to her Lean Cuisine."

"And her adorable boys," said Sherry as Day headed for the door. "Do you like children, Mr. Beltway?"

"Harry. Please call me Harry. Yes, I guess. Sometimes I don't think I'm real comfortable around them. I was an only child."

"Ah, just like our Timmy."

"Timmy?"

"A—a cat. Our cat, right, honey?" said Duncannon, thrashing around to catch the waiter's attention. "Now, Harry, I'm going to place an order for a dessert that will knock your socks off. Grand Marnier soufflé—nothing better. Except you've got to give them enough notice."

"Mr. Beltway—uh, Harry," said Sherry, giggling coquettishly. "Tell me more about your childhood."

I spent the next few days thinking about whether I really wanted to work for another campaign. Ever.

_____

Day Duncannon asked if I would just come into the office for a day: Once I saw the Duncannon campaign in action, she said, I would know how much they needed me.

So I showed up one crisp October afternoon and went awkwardly from desk to desk, introducing myself. Five Duncannon brothers were there: The family liked to hang together. They were a close, rowdy, *physical* family. They punched each other and everyone else. When they first met you, there was a short little punch to the shoulder. If they really liked you, you got a noogie, the old knuckles to the temple. Their heartiest move, the headlock with a sock to the gut, was reserved for childhood pals from the neighborhood. Since there were so many of them, it seemed that there was at least one Duncannon in every room of the office at any time. They helped out—running errands, licking envelopes, cheering brother Mike's speeches, and discouraging anyone foolish enough to heckle the family candidate.

The campaign was in the first throes of volunteer growth, so no one really had time for me. They were too busy training new recruits, mostly cute young college girls Day liked to call "popsies."

Walking from the coffee machine into the conference room in the late morning, I was surprised to find the shades down and the lights dimmed. I stood quietly in the back, but Sam Magillicuddy spotted me and swooped over.

"Listen up, everybody. Before I continue, let me introduce someone I hope will become a valuable new addition to our team." Sam put a beefy arm around my shoulder. "This is Harry. We're trying to recruit him as Director of Christian Relations."

He leaned close and whispered in my ear, "Harry, this is one of the great things about these orientation sessions. You get to sit in a dark room with a bunch of cute popsies. Pick your seat right, Harry, and you just may get lucky tonight." I turned to find a place to sit, and in a single energetic bound Sam was back at the front of the room.

"Now, ladies, you all know why you're here. Your mission, should you choose to accept it, is to get our candidate into the White House. What stands in our way is the other guys. But first, and more important, is our own guys. Let's see who you're up against. This is the opposition. Bill, let's have the first slide."

A picture of General Orville Clayton flashed onto the screen.

"A light-skinned African-American war hero. Our worst nightmare. Black people like him because he's black. White people like him because he's not too black. But fortunately he really doesn't stand a chance. You know why? Because he's black. This is America, after all."

One of the more nervy popsies piped up, probably an Agnes Scott girl. "But I heard the *Newsweek* polls say he's ahead."

"Don't bother your pretty head about *Newsweek*, little lady. Bill Cosby had a top-rated TV show, but nobody was about to elect him president, either. Pretty soon your Orville Clayton will be peddling Jell-O Pudding Pops right next to the Cos.

"Next. Lemuel Atwater." A dude in slicked hair and a rumpled, oversized flannel shirt popped into view. "A real clothes horse, that one. If there was a country club set in the north woods of Maine, he would be their idol. If he gets elected, every day will be dress-down Friday. You'll get a plaid shirt with your birth certificate or citizenship papers. Lemuel wants to rename the United States the United Colors of Benetton. He is tolerant and good and civic-minded, a real Boy Scout who thinks community involvement is the highest ideal of the nation." Sam paused. "So I think we'll let ol' Lem get back to his bumpkin community while the rest of us get on with the business of the nation. Next slide, if you please."

A bearded black man appeared on the screen.

"Now who the hell is that?" Sam paused and scratched his head, the image of genuine befuddlement. "Wait a minute, Bill, can you shift the projector a little? You're cutting off the bottom of the slide. Ah, I see now. The feet. That's Claude Locke. He believes the moral fabric of America is slowly wearing away, and that he's the key to our salvation. He's a very smart guy, well-educated, articulate, but crazy as a loon. Think Clarence Thomas on acid. The brother from another planet. He hasn't got a chance."

Arnold Schwarzenegger appeared on the screen. Titters went up from the audience.

"Arnie, it's not your time." Sam put on a dreadful Austrian accent. "*HASTA LA VISTA, BABY. I'LL BE BA-A-ACK.* You know, the day he and Maria Shriver decide to run, we may be in serious trouble. Next slide, please.

"Orson Kane. Trillionaire Fabergé egg-collecting smirking scion of a liberal publishing empire. Flat tax. Fat chance!

"Now the Big Kahuna himself, Bill Pineapple, the Don Ho of politics. Another war hero, but older and lighter. War Hero Lite. More promise, less fulfilling. You can't believe it's not the real thing. I would like to brief you on Bill's positions, but until he decides what they are himself, we'll just have to wait. We can't underestimate him, but we can't really get a hold of him either. It's like fighting fog.

"And, last but not least, the Toadster. Toad Gecko. Speaker of the House. Rabble-rouser. Thorn in the current administration's side. Our big unknown. He's done more to shake up American politics than anyone else in recent years, but nobody knows whether to take him seriously. He's apparently set down his thinking in his latest book, but nobody seems to have read it. If any of you wants to volunteer . . ."

Mike Duncannon took it for granted that I would sign on. I wasn't so sure. I liked him—I liked him a lot—but I couldn't see where it would lead, how it fit into my career, such as it was. Some big decisions just seem to make themselves, though. The expectations and assumptions close in until you look around and realize that circumstance has made up your mind for you.

"Harry, come on out to the house and have dinner with Sherry and me," Duncannon said, putting his arm around my shoulder and shepherding me toward the door. "Give us a chance to talk things over like just plain folks."

I knew that if I got into that car my fate would be sealed. "Well—" I said, but he wouldn't let me finish.

"I'll call Sherry and tell her to set another place. Do you like corned beef and cabbage?"

"I love corned beef and cabbage." I hate corned beef and cabbage.

"Then it's settled."

We talked idly of this and that during the short drive. How the whole region has changed since he grew up here. The movie theaters that have folded. The neighborhoods that have gone up or down.

"It's not the way it was, Harry. It's not the way it was. I grew up surrounded by my kind of people, all beating the be-jeesus out of each other, in a friendly sort of way. *Sic transit gloria mundi*, Harry. You know: *There goes the neighborhood*."

I worked up the courage to touch on a sore point. "A lot of people say you're racist, Mr. Duncannon."

"Racist? Racist?" He punched the air with his fist. "There was a Negro in my school, Harry. Nobody mistreated him any worse than we mistreated each other. I've always liked the Negro people. We had a couple of Negro servants when I was little, and they were fine, upstanding folks. *Uncle Remus* was my family's favorite reading when I was a youngster, and I could do a pretty fair colored accent, too."

He opened his eyes wide and wiggled his fingers in the air. " 'Tu'n me loose, fo' I kick de natal stuffin' outen you.' I really admired the way those people talked—had kind of a ring to it."

That certainly didn't sound racist to me.

"I like blacks and Jews individually, Harry. It's just whole big groups of them all coming into my neighborhood at once that I mind. Whether it's wetbacks crossing the Rio Grande or the coloreds moving into nice Irish Catholic neighborhoods, it just isn't right." He pounded his right fist into his beefy left palm. "Remind me to show you my barbed-wire collection some time, Harry. Barbed wire is one of the great American inventions—barbed wire, razor wire, concertina wire—great stuff. I had an uncle who made his own barbed wire. In the evenings the whole family sat in the parlor, listening to the radio, twisting the little barbs together." He dabbed a nostalgic tear from his eye and laughed gently. "Sort of the Duncannon version of a quilting party. There ought to be more of that, Harry—families gathering together in the evening, making things with their own hands, forging better neighborhoods through walls and wire."

Duncannon's house in McLean was a comfortable, white-painted brick affair. It was surrounded, of course, by a very high wall with barbed wire and broken glass on the top.

"My wife picked out the glass, Harry. It's Steuben."

Sherry met us at the door. She hugged and kissed him and smiled as though she lived only for the moment when he came home. "How was your day?" she asked.

"Day's just fine. Best cousin a guy's ever had," he replied. "How is *your* cousin?" He had obviously told some variant of this joke about six thousand times, but both of them laughed. A sort of wider, less funny, more Catholic Burns and Allen. I thought if ever I'd seen the incarnation of family values, Mike and Sherry Duncannon were it.

We ensconced ourselves in his study as Sherry disappeared into the kitchen. "Tell me all about yourself, Harry," he said. Sherry brought a couple of beers and a plate of deviled ham spread on Ritz crackers. She brought his slippers and traded his tie and jacket for a baggy cardigan. With each passing minute I felt the world of high-powered Washington fade while Middle America took on form and substance before my eyes.

"You watch much TV, Harry?" he asked.

"I've never had a lot of time for it."

"You should. Very American. TV and movies—you can learn a lot about life from TV and movies. Ever see 'All in the Family'?"

"Once or twice."

"Great show," he said. "That Archie Bunker. I wish I could find myself a running mate like that. Then I'd have this whole campaign sewed up. You know, I once thought of asking Carroll O'Connor to come on board. But then he got that other show—you know, the one with the black guy. And what kind of name is 'Carroll,' anyway? Back in my neighborhood we would have beat up somebody with a name like that. I don't care if he's called O'Connor or not.

"How about 'Mr. Ed,' Harry?"

"I saw some reruns." I couldn't imagine where this conversation was going.

"I'll let you in on a little secret, Harry. One of my little tricks, back when I was a speechwriter, was pretending I was writing lines for Mr. Ed. Especially when I was writing speeches for Agnew. It really helped me focus. Think Mr. Ed, and you get the perfect Agnew."

"I never thought of that. There is a certain resemblance."

"Okay, Harry. 'Gilligan's Island.' Which one did you prefer? Ginger or Mary Ann?"

I never had been able to decide. Fortunately I was rescued from this admission of uncertainty by The Call.

Once Duncannon was in his Barcalounger he preferred to stay there. He reached over and flipped on the speakerphone. "Hello, Duncannon here."

"Mike, this is Donald Degan. How are you?"

Duncannon almost shot out of his chair. You could see that his father and the Catholic schools had trained him well. He respected his elders as automatically as he breathed.

"Mr. President, it's wonderful to hear from you. How are you?"

"Well, Mike, I'm feeling fine. Jenny says I've started forgetting things, but I haven't noticed it."

"Ah, Mr. President, forgive me for mentioning it, but Jenny was your *first* wife."

"Is that so? My, my, things sure are happening fast nowadays."

Duncannon laughed good-naturedly. "Yes, sir, they are."

"So how's your wife and child, Mike? You do have a child, right?"

Duncannon looked acutely uncomfortable, but he always knew how to change the subject, to get unwanted digressions back on track. "I know how busy you are, Mr. President. I realize you didn't take the time to call just to socialize. What can I do for you?"

There was a very long silence. I began to think Degan had fallen asleep or been disconnected.

"Well, Mike," Degan began at last, "You know how much I like you. Everybody likes you. You're a wonderful human being. Quite likable. Salt of the earth. But I got a call from Gordy Hedge a little while ago. And he's not the first one to call. He's

not even the second one to call. Or the third. Or the fourth."
He trailed off again as though wondering where to go next.
There was another long silence.

"Yes, Mr. President?" Duncannon said gently. "Gordy
Hedge called to say what?"

"Well, you know Gordy was not happy about you running
against him in '88 and '92. I don't know if I told you this at
the time, Mike, but I wasn't too happy either. You know, my
motto—my Eleventh Commandment—has always been 'Speak
no evil of thy fellow Republicans,' and you were not being very
nice to old Gordy. And now he's worried that you're being
awfully negative about Pineapple. Some folks worry that you're
splitting the party."

"I'm just sticking up for what I believe in, Mr. President,
and I know how much you respect that."

"Yes, I do, Mike. I certainly do."

"Well, Mr. President, how would you advise me to proceed?" Duncannon asked.

"Ahhhhh, well—uhhhhh—hmmmm."

"You know how I admire you, sir. I've even taken the liberty
of implying that I would be proud if folks thought of me as the
Donald Degan of '96."

"Well, that's very flattering, Mike. But then who would I
be?"

"I've always loved your sense of humor, Mr. President,"
Duncannon said, then laughed. "But tell me what to do. I
value your opinions as no one else's."

"Ahhhh, well—ahhhhhhh, Mike—ahhhhhh, I can't think of
anything to say right at the moment. Can you give me a little

help here? You always were the best darn speechwriter around."

"Help? Of course I can help, Mr. President. Tell you what, if you want to hang up and wait a few minutes I'll bang out a script and fax it to you. Then call me back and we'll have a great conversation."

A moment later Duncannon was pounding the keys of an old Royal manual typewriter. "Word processors may be great, Harry, but I still love these old things. You know, the phrase 'Silent Majority' first rolled out of this very machine."

The words flowed. Within five minutes Duncannon was feeding three pages of clean dialogue into his fax machine. One minute later the telephone rang.

"Mike, this is Donald Degan calling. How are you?" The former president's voice was strong, clear, confident.

"Fine, Mr. President. What can I do for you?"

"Mike, our party is in trouble. I look around and wonder where we are going."

"Yes, Mr. President. I agree with your sentiments one hundred percent."

"Mike, have we lost track of our boots, and lost track of—"

"Excuse me, Mr. President, that's 'roots,' not 'boots.' It must have gotten blurred in the fax."

"Oh, of course. Sorry." Degan cleared his throat and started again. "Mike, have we lost track of our roots, and lost track of our direction? We fought Communism around the globe, tried to make the world safe so that people everywhere could live free and proud. But now, we ourselves, right here in America, live economically hemmed in on all sides. Some people are ashamed of our own country. How have we come to this state, Mike Duncannon?"

"I think it's the Democrats, sir."

"Mike Duncannon, a challenge lies ahead of us. It's not only Jeb and Susan Clanton and their crew. Our own party has stumbled, Mike. Our party is the Grand Old Party, but sometimes, as we get old—and I was born in 1911, so I know what I'm talking about—as we get old, there comes a time when we must pass the reins to younger hands, to quick minds, to someone who knows the way. I realized that several years ago. I can think of a few others in our party who might follow my lead and give some thought to retiring gracefully."

"What direction do you think our country should take, Mr. President?"

"We must recapture our national birthright, Mike Duncannon. Helping others is the Christian way, and America gives more to the world than anyone else, but first we must tend to our own house. We need to patch the walls. We need to clean out the dirt and stench. We need to tell those guests who have overstayed their welcome that it's time to get out. We need to fill our house with prayer and song, and all pitch in to work together, shoulder to shoulder, as one strong family."

"I couldn't agree with you more, Mr. President."

The president's voice grew softer again. "That was very nice, Mike."

"It was your advice, Mr. President. I thank you. I can't tell you how much I value your thoughts."

"Well, you've always been a big help to me, Mike. Just remember, as long as I'm president there will always be a place for you in the administration."

"Uh, actually, Mr. President, I'm running for president myself, if you recall."

"Ohhhh. Well, I wish you a lot of luck, Mike. You certainly have my vote."

Duncannon flipped off the speakerphone, took a long drink of his beer, and turned to me with a smile. "That was a wonderful endorsement from former President Degan, Harry. You might want to take a few excerpts from this telephone conversation here and make sure they get over to the wire services." He handed me his script. Then he paused. "Assuming, of course, that you're in."

At that moment Sherry entered the room with the next course of appetizers: pigs in blankets and celery stuffed with peanut butter.

"Are you joining the team, Harry?" she asked.

Duncannon looked at me and said, "Can we welcome you aboard?"

"Well, I've been tempted to get back into politics." Everything felt right. I felt like I was home.

"A pig in a blanket, Harry?" Sherry asked, holding out the plate. She gazed at me fondly as I took one. "Mike's going to win, you know. My Mikey's going to be president."

"Yes, Harry, we're going all the way this time. Are you coming with us?"

I was in.

2

My desk was near the Mod Squad, two men and a woman who had been hired about two weeks before me. Everyone called them that, and although I wasn't sure, I suspected they might have coined it themselves.

"One Black, one Blonde, one Jew," explained Gary Miller, who was in charge of media. Peggy Linden was the blonde, an attractive woman in her early thirties who looked like a model for J. Crew. She often went braless, wore big silver earrings, and favored clogs and high suede boots. In short, she could easily pass as a liberal, and that was her job. She monitored events and media—a lot of listening to NPR—and kept the Duncannon campaign abreast of all the liberal bogeymen haunting the voters of America. She was the office expert on what we called the "perms"—the permanent press, the reporters who could make or break a campaign.

Horace Johnson was the Oreo. He had worked for Degan and Hedge, rising to become an assistant to the assistant of somebody in the Education Department before the Clantons had come to town. Now he ran his own consulting firm, combining his conservative values with all the multicultural gobbledygook that corporations pay lots of money for nowadays. Horace was the type of person I could understand, someone not unlike myself. He tried to avoid politics, but he was addicted. When Duncannon approached him to be, as he put it, "token nigger," he couldn't resist. He followed the whole racism issue and figured out how to spin Duncannon into a more moderate orbit in case we really had a shot at the candidacy. His desk sported a handwritten sign that read: "Horace Johnson, Head Zulu."

And who was the Wandering Jew? Barry Orenstein, a guy so nervous he practically never sat down. He specialized in the religious right, too—Orthodox Jews who might actually go for Duncannon's emphasis on family values and fiscal responsibility. "Of course, there's the Israeli thing," he said to me the first week I was there. "Most Jews hate him. But we're working on it. You know, Duncannon was very pro-Israeli during the Yom Kippur War."

"Been a lot Manischewitz over the dam since that one, my friend," said Horace, winking at me.

Barry was a stats man, a lawyer who had left Davis Polk because he hated big business. His specialty, self-taught, was the focus group and the analysis of exit polls. It was really only in his spare time that the others let him work on the Jew question, which most of us thought was a lost cause. Every once in a while his mother would call from Brooklyn and tell him she was sitting *shiva* for him. A son who would work for Duncannon was no better than a dog—he might as well be dead. The calls always seemed to cheer him up.

The two other Mod Squadders were insanely jealous that

Horace got to attend the Million Man March. He reported back the next day, still dressed in a dashiki.

"Duncannon-Farrakhan . . . *that's* the ticket," Horace said, laughing.

The most serious challenge to Duncannon's bid for the nomination, of course, was Toad Gecko, the "Croaker of the House," as Mike liked to call him, "the man with a lily pad for a political platform," the Big Hopper, Amphibius Rex, the guy who had leapfrogged from nowhere to everywhere in hardly any time at all. Gecko had taken the party by storm, put Jeb Clanton on the run. The public either loved him or loved to hate him. Everybody expected his next move to be a bid for the presidency. He was the one person who really worried us, because he drew his constituency from the same group of whacko, ultraconservative, flag-waving, antigovernment malcontents as Duncannon.

But Gecko's announcement didn't come. He spent a lot of time back home, staying away from reporters. When people did catch up to him and ask about his intentions, he gave some cryptic, noncommittal reply, which was not like Gecko at all. It was a complete metamorphosis, people said, except he went backward, the toad turning into a little tadpole. And then all of a sudden Gecko just up and disappeared. One day you couldn't get away from him, the next day nobody knew where he was. Some people figured he had been abducted by aliens, or at least that he'd been given a steady gig as an alien on "Star Trek," his favorite show, and was off being fitted for his pointy ears and custom nose wrinkles.

Duncannon, though, knew Gecko well enough to be sure he would be back. "We'll hear from Gecko, Harry. You mark my words."

He was right. But the Gecko we heard from was not Toad. It was Brandy, his lesbian activist sister.

Our first campaign headquarters was in an old sporting goods store near the Capitol. There was a basketball hoop hung up out back where Duncannon and his brothers used to take on all comers. On those long summer evenings they would play almost until dark, then they'd sit out on the front stoop sipping lemonade, before heading down to Sholl's Cafeteria for dinner. Some of the popsies finally set up a lemonade stand on the street, which gave just the right all-American image and brought in a little extra cash. They put up a big sign that read "Duncannon's Fresh-Squeezed Lemonade," and under it a little sign that said: "It's not Pineapple."

Down in the basement Duncannon hung a punching bag. He went down there almost every day and gave it a few hundred with the left and a couple hundred with the right, just like Pop taught him. When he was in a bad mood he'd take a picture of Jeb Clanton or Bill Pineapple or whoever was getting on his nerves at the time and tack it onto that bag. By the time he was finished they'd be reduced to paper pulp, ready for recycling.

I was sitting in the office on the day the Gecko fiasco began, concentrating on one of the new popsies, trying to figure out how to angle myself so that I could see between the buttons of her blouse without her noticing. Suddenly the door burst open. In charged a woman who might have been attractive but for the butch haircut, Buddy Holly spectacles, combat boots, and a look that implied she would rip the balls right off any man who looked at her funny. I crossed my legs instinctively.

"Where's Duncannon?" she demanded.

"He's not available, Ms-s-s-s-s." I caught myself just in time before saying "Miss"—my life would have ended right then and there. But I wound up sounding like a mosquito impersonator.

"Make him available."

"I'm afraid I don't know who you are. . . ." This time I just trailed off, not having a clue what to call her.

"Brandy Gecko."

Oh, shit. Whatever this meant, it wasn't good.

"Ah, and what brings you to Washington, Ms-s-s-s-s—Ms. Gecko?"

She hopped up onto the edge of my desk and leaned over, much closer than I liked. "Get me Duncannon."

I went to get Duncannon. He had worked up a good sweat down there in the basement. He had a picture of some Fortune 500 CEO who had recently laid off a couple thousand workers, which made the value of his own stock options rocket to the moon. Duncannon was giving the snooty bastard one in the jaw for every single one of those workers.

"Brandy Gecko's here to see you," I said.

I thought Duncannon was going to pass out. His face went from bright red to dead pale and he took a half step back. "*Brandy* Gecko? The *funny* one? I'm not going to see her, Harry, she's got cooties."

"I don't think she's going to leave unless she sees you."

"What does she want?" I don't remember ever seeing Duncannon look so intimidated by anyone.

"I don't know," I said.

Day Duncannon had been working away at her own little punching bag over in the corner. "I'll talk to her, Mike," she said, taking off her ten-ounce pink boxing gloves and pushing the hair out of her eyes. "Harry, come with me."

I was worried. I wished some of the Duncannon brothers were around, but they had made themselves scarce during the past few weeks. I was afraid all hell would break loose up there, and the prospect of getting between Brandy Gecko and Day Duncannon all by myself made my stomach churn.

"You're Brandy Gecko?" Day said with a cordial but nononsense smile. "I'm Day Duncannon, Mike's sister and campaign manager. What can I do for you?"

"I want my brother back."

"I didn't think you liked your brother very much."

"I don't, but if it's a choice between your sonofabitch cousin and my sonofabitch brother, I'll take mine."

"I can understand that. We Duncannons were always taught to stick together. There's family, and then there's everyone else."

Brandy Gecko softened a little. "I think maybe we can understand each other. We're a lot alike."

Day recoiled in horror. "Oh, no, we're not."

"I mean, we're both feminists."

"Speak for yourself. I'm no feminist. All I ever wanted was a nice husband and to stay home with the kids."

Brandy looked surprised. "But you've had your career. You were Treasurer of the United States."

"Look, lady—if that's what you are—I'm a single mother and I *have* to work. Some women work in fast-food restaurants and some women are Treasurer of the United States. And what makes you think it's such a great job, anyway, sitting there signing all those dollar bills, day after day?"

"Oh, I didn't know you signed them individually."

"Lloyd Bentsen probably doesn't, but *I* did when I was treasurer. I take pride in my work. That's the problem with America today, nobody's willing to roll up their sleeves and get their hands dirty. But that's what a Duncannon presidency will bring back to this country. . . ."

She was on a roll. Once she got started like this she could keep going for hours, and she would get so worked up we'd have to peel her off the wall. Brandy Gecko started to look like a steamroller was driving very slowly back and forth over her head.

"Can we get back to the subject of my brother?" she said.

"Your brother," Day said with a hint of disgust. "Your brother, your brother. Your brother is all anyone talked about for most of the last year. I think the nation deserves a little rest." She paused a moment, looking perplexed. "But, you know, it sure isn't like him to be so quiet. Hell's bells, what has he been doing with himself? He hasn't croaked, has he?" She laughed uproariously.

"He's not doing anything with himself. I think somebody else has done something with him, and I want him back."

"Back? What do you mean, back?"

"Toad has disappeared. I think he's been kidnapped."

"Who would kidnap Toad Gecko? Have you ever read *The*

Ransom of Red Chief? If anybody ever kidnapped your brother, how would they bear up under the torment? What on earth would they do with him?"

"I hoped Mike Duncannon could tell me that."

Day Duncannon pretended to be nonchalant, but the visit from Gecko's sister shook her up. Long after everyone else had gone home, she sat at her desk, staring straight into space.

"Day? Is everything okay?" I asked on my way out.

"I hope so. I have an awful sick feeling about this Gecko thing. Something seems kinda fishy." Day reached into her bottom desk drawer and brought out a flask. "Harry—let's drink to the wonderful world of politics."

I accepted the flask from her and downed its contents. Vodka. Not bad—must have been Stoli or Finlandia. Certainly not American.

"Day is so unusual. Is it your real name?" I said.

"No. My real name is Annette. When I was little, I was very dark, with dark brown eyes, and Pop used to say I looked just like a little dago. But cousin Mike, who lived right next door, was only three years old, and he couldn't say 'dago,' so he would just say 'Day.' After a while it stuck, and I've been using it ever since. Guess Toad Gecko and I have a lot in common."

"How's that?"

"Well, his sister told me how he got his name. I had never known. A family thing, just like me. One of his cousins couldn't say his real name, Todd, so it came out Toad. You know, Harry, I don't want to sound like I'm getting soft, but I felt real bad for her. I know how I would feel if someone kidnapped my cousin Mike, even if I do want to kill him six or seven times a day."

With New Hampshire only months away, we started concentrating on the strengths and weaknesses of all the candidates. Barry Orenstein briefed us frequently on the data he was gathering. One thing that particularly bothered him was how few people outside of Washington even knew about Mike Duncannon.

"Name recognition is the first thing we need with the great unwashed public," he told us one day, stroking his closely trimmed beard. "Names are the name of the game. If the name Cheez-Whiz was put on the ballot, you can bet lots of people would vote for it, just because they've heard of it and it makes them feel kind of warm and runny inside. Now *we're* at a disadvantage. Pineapple they know. If not as a candidate, as a fruit. Nobody's not heard of pineapple. And Kane is a magazine, and Kane's father used to get in the papers riding around on a motorcycle like some geriatric delinquent, or putting all his hot air into a balloon and dropping himself into the ocean. Folks remember the name, whether they know why or not. But Duncannon? What's a Duncannon? A kind of towel, maybe? Who is Duncannon? Does it have one 'n' or two?"

We kicked around ideas, tried to get Mike more coverage, and began the monumental task of trying to *control* our loose cannon candidate.

Peggy taped all our opponents' speeches, which came in handy when developing opposition, or oppo, strategies. Bill Pineapple, always the strong, silent type, made a definite move for the cripple vote late in the fall. Obviously his advisers had told him he had to open up about his war injuries. The results were pretty hilarious. It was late on a cold Friday afternoon, and we were all feasting on popcorn when we dissected Pineapple's latest attempt to get down with the people:

"My disability, which I suffered for the good of my country, has forced me to use button hooks. I resisted it for a long time, but finally I realized that I should not refuse the help that was offered to me; I should not feel ashamed. And I found that button hooks saved me time, made my life richer. So I would say to all of you, use button hooks. If you need them. Or use them even if you don't need them, because they might save you time. Too often, when we talk about politics, when we talk about the government, we only think of the big things, like taxes and foreign affairs and the like. But what do we, as Americans, as people, spend most of our time doing? We spend our time doing little things, like buttoning buttons and making toast and trying to fit our keys into that little hole in the doorknob. So I want to tell you today that, as your president, I will dedicate my energy toward making your lives easier. Not just the big things in life, like your jobs and health care and safety on the streets, but the little things as well. I will make sure that everybody has a button hook. We will bring back those little alligator clips that hold your mittens on your sleeves so they don't get lost. Bibs so that you don't look ridiculous after every meal with food all over your best shirt."

Duncannon had come into the room at the beginning of Pineapple's tirade and soon started smirking. "Hey, I think he should send some of those button hooks to Lemuel Atwater. He needs 'em for those Howdy Doody shirts he wears all the time."

Pineapple was a real problem. What he lacked in charisma, he made up for in longevity and connections. Here was a guy who couldn't talk his way out of a paper bag, and yet he was the front-running candidate.

"I used to hate to write speeches for that bastard, back when I worked for Dick Nixon," Duncannon groused. "He's got no soul. Even my words couldn't make him look good, and a guy's in trouble when my blarney doesn't work."

Duncannon took great pride in penning all of his speeches himself. He could work anywhere—on planes, in buses, in bed right before he dozed off. And he didn't need any special electronic equipment. Number two pencils and yellow legal pads were the American way. "Laptops—they're like computer masturbation. They're sinful, they make you go blind!" he told me one night on a plane to Columbus, winking as he settled down to create more hyperbole.

He would run what he referred to as "the final draft" of a speech past me or Barry Orenstein before he spoke, but what he said up on the platform usually bore no resemblance to what had been in the script, and it often left us unprepared for press fallout. It became a game between Barry and me to rate the various embellishments on the stump from one to ten. One day, when Duncannon was riffing on our American forefathers, he invented a liturgical cant—call it "Simple Solutions to Complex Modern Problems":

"And what would our forefathers do with criminals?"

"Lock and load, blast 'em dead," the crowd roared back.

"And what would they do with homosexuals?"

"Lock and load, blast 'em dead!"

"It's a ten," said Barry, reaching for his Maalox tablets.

The crowds were amazing. I looked out at them and felt like I was living in a Frank Capra movie. They were wholesome, and yet they were angry. Mike gave them the release they needed to face their lousy lives. Every day, the crowds got bigger. Duncannon egged them on, getting them to yell "Mix it up, Mike" and "Lock and load!" at every appearance.

"Why is our country TOPS?" he asked an enthusiastic audience at a Christian Academy in Nashville. "Our country, our culture, is TOPS because we're Christians. We're white Christians, and that's the best damn thing to be in the whole world. Because it is the true religion, and ours is the only true country." The crowd went wild, and Barry went white to the lips.

"We'll build a wall around our country to hold back the waves of immigrants beating against our shores. What's more, we'll put a *roof* over our country to keep those immigrants from flying in. Walls and a roof—that's home sweet home."

"Home sweet home!" the crowd echoed in jubilation.

"But you know what we'll put in that roof?" Duncannon went on, his voice dropping low. "You know what that roof needs? It needs a chimney. Why does it need a chimney? It needs a hearth for the family to gather 'round."

"The family! The family!" shouted the audience.

"But *more* important," Duncannon roared, "*most* important of all, we need a chimney for Santa Claus to come down. My friends, when I am president, Santa Claus will no longer have to fear the ACLU and their godless pals. He will bring his presents to all good little Christian girls and boys without interference!"

"Santa Claus! Santa Claus!"

"This is great," I said. "Look at the crowds we're getting. I wish the perms would start to follow us more seriously."

"Be careful what you wish for. You just might get it," said Barry.

I began to see reasons for Barry's cynicism. Our candidate really did seem like a loose cannon. No matter how carefully we plotted strategies, we never knew from one day to the next what he would do when he got up on stage. There were times when I genuinely thought Duncannon had lost his mind. But he knew his audience better than I did. He got the response he was looking for.

Not long after I joined the Duncannon team, we were stumping in New York, where a lot of his rhetoric didn't play too well and the political machine was outright hostile. So he switched his approach. Standing on a temporary stage on the first-base line of a high school baseball field in White Plains, he proceeded to entertain the masses.

"You know," he told the crowd—surprisingly large, given the political climate, which, like the weather, was cool and damp. "I like debates. I don't think you really get the full picture when you see candidates talking in a vacuum. You want to see them in action. You want to see how they really stack up against each other. So I asked some of my opponents to come here today, so we could discuss the issues in front of you." The audience looked surprised. Was this really true?

"But they wouldn't come," Duncannon said. "No, they were too busy someplace else to be here with you." Whether this was true or not, the audience felt slighted. "They were too busy. Well, I'm not too busy. I cleared my whole afternoon just to come here and talk to you folks. But I feel bad that you get cheated out of a good old-fashioned honest debate, so I'm going to give you one anyway."

The audience was charmed in spite of itself. And befuddled. Duncannon paused, looked around, smiled.

"I've created my own versions of some of the other candidates. I tried to reproduce them as accurately as possible. So let's see here."

He began rummaging through a big duffel bag behind the podium. He took out a tank of compressed helium, fitted the neck of a large balloon over the nozzle, and twisted the valve.

"Now, Orson Kane. Orson Kane sometimes needs a little time to get pumped up for his appearances." Duncannon hummed "If I Were a Rich Man" as the balloon inflated, growing larger and larger to reveal a pair of round spectacles drawn on in marker.

"Okay, now—Harry, will you hold this a moment?" I grabbed the neck of the balloon while he plunged back into his duffel bag. He produced a small cassette tape recorder tied to the end of a string. He took the balloon from me and wrapped the string tightly around its neck.

"Now, Mr. Kane," Duncannon said, looking sternly at the balloon. "A lot of people in this country aren't feeling too happy these days. They work hard, real hard, but then all their money goes to the government and goes overseas. What do you think about that?"

He pushed the button on the tape recorder, then released the balloon. It rose quickly skyward. At the same time the recorder began squawking in a loud, cartoonish voice: "17 PERCENT FLAT TAX . . . 17 PERCENT FLAT TAX . . . 17 PERCENT FLAT TAX . . ."

"Well, now, Mr. Kane," Duncannon said in a conversational tone. "I can see your point, but aren't there other issues to consider?"

"17 PERCENT FLAT TAX . . . 17 PERCENT FLAT TAX . . . 17 PERCENT FLAT TAX . . ."

"I think you're getting a little carried away with that one idea, Mr. Kane," Duncannon said. "Mr. Kane?" The recorded voice grew fainter and fainter as the balloon rose higher and drifted away. Duncannon looked at the audience and shrugged. "Ah, well, I guess he got his money's worth. I think he was really just in it for the ride."

Duncannon turned back to his duffel bag and rooted around again. He brought out a pineapple and laid it on the floor. The audience laughed a little. That one was obvious. Duncannon remembered something and retrieved it from the bag. "The pen!" He jabbed a ball-point pen into the left side of the pineapple.

"Ooooh," the audience groaned. It was so bad it was good.

"Lemuel?" Duncannon called into the duffel bag. "Lemuel

Atwater, where are you? We can't find you, Lemuel Atwater. Oh, there you are." He came out with a Howdy Doody puppet, clad in a red-and-black plaid shirt. "Howdy doody, Lem Atwater."

The audience cracked up.

"Okay, now let the debate begin." He glanced skyward. "Maybe Mr. Kane will decide to rejoin us when he gets tired of the jet-set crowd up there. Now—who would like to go first?" And he proceeded to play all the parts: Pineapple slow and creaky, Atwater a glib but dizzy dummy.

PINEAPPLE: I have ideas. Lots of ideas.

ATWATER: I have ideas, too.

PINEAPPLE: I haven't told you many of my ideas yet, but I'm going to start telling them real soon.

ATWATER: I have better ideas.

PINEAPPLE: I have experience and ideas.

ATWATER: I have really, really fabulous ideas.

DUNCANNON: Boys, boys—why don't we talk about some of these ideas?

ATWATER: Hey, good idea, Mr. Duncannon. Why didn't we think of that? What kinds of ideas do you think we should talk about?

DUNCANNON: Well, the ideas that concern these people here. Like jobs and the economy. Like their children's education. Like medical care, and what they're looking forward to when they get old, and what kind of world will be waiting for their children, and their children's children. Like how we can keep America great, and how we can deal fairly with the rest of the world—*fairly*—without just letting other countries take advantage of us because we've always tried to be open and to lend a hand where it's needed.

ATWATER: My ideas are better than yours.

DUNCANNON: Let's not just have negative campaigning here.

ATWATER: I'm younger than Pineapple.

PINEAPPLE: I used to be young. I was young in World War Two, when I fought for our country. I was young back when we knew what being young was really all about.

ATWATER: I can come up with any ideas these nice people want.

DUNCANNON: Don't you think the people want a candidate with firm ideas, ones he sticks by?

ATWATER: I've got firm ideas, too. You want firm, sticky ideas, I've got firm, sticky ideas. I can tell you what they are, sometime, too.

PINEAPPLE: I have very strong ideas.

DUNCANNON: I'm very glad to hear that, Senator. I do, too, as these people know. I like a man of convictions. Tell me, what are your convictions?

PINEAPPLE: Well, I believe in up.

DUNCANNON: Up?

PINEAPPLE: Absolutely. Up. Down, too. I also believe in down.

DUNCANNON: I see.

ATWATER: I'm not sure I would agree with that. Up and down are kind of extreme. I think we have to explore the middle ground. See if there isn't some other route that might be more suitable.

PINEAPPLE: I believe in left and right, too. (Pause.) Though I sometimes have a hard time telling them apart.

ATWATER: He's losing it.

PINEAPPLE: I'm in fine shape. I can run up stairs two at a time. I can do jumping jacks.

Duncannon began bouncing the pineapple on his palm. It fell to the ground with a splat.

The rest of his speech was clear sailing. The audience loved him.

Our campaign was certainly getting attention. But we were getting attention from unwanted followers as well.

The CEO Bomber made his first appearance on November 2—Duncannon's fifty-seventh birthday. It had been a crappy morning of pounding the halls of Congress, trying to rustle up support. The message was loud and clear wherever we went: We love you, Mike, you're a swell guy, but there's no way in hell we want you as president of the United States.

"I say what they think, but they don't want to hear it," Duncannon said in the car on the way to headquarters. "The people agree with me. Hell, Harry, anybody in his right mind has to agree with me. We can't keep giving away our country and expect to have anything left, and we can't flush all moral values down the toilet and then turn around and wonder why there's so much crime."

Duncannon was thinking about New York. He was flying up there late in the afternoon. Day had set up dinner with the mayor and paved the way for a one-on-one with the governor the following morning. New York did not like Mike Duncannon, and Mike Duncannon was none too fond of New York. He would not be playing to the sort of crowds he enjoyed, and he was trying to wrap his mind around the challenge of getting the support he so desperately needed.

Headquarters was dead quiet. Two or three popsies lounged at their desks, but the normal bustle was missing.

"Where is everybody?" Duncannon yelled when he arrived. "It's *next* November that you all get to go home—AFTER I win the election!"

Lights flashed on, streamers flew, horns blew. "Happy birthday, Mike Duncannon!" shouted a hundred voices as the campaign staff bubbled out from under desks and through doorways.

Duncannon loved a party. The bigger and noisier, the better. Preoccupied though he was with New York, he enjoyed himself. Everybody knew there was little time for play, so it was a party on the run—deli platter, mounds of cole slaw and potato salad, a huge cake in the shape of the White House with the letters, "Happy Birthday, Mike: It's Yours!"

For presents he got a pineapple corer, a plaid shirt, a subscription to *Kane* magazine, a piece of antique Frentress "Split Diamond" barbed wire strung near Robert Lee, Texas, by General Winfield Scott himself, the first of the new run of "Duncannon for President" T-shirts signed by everyone in the campaign office, a Jeb Clanton toilet paper holder, and a few actually useful items.

"Open the big one!" said one of the popsies. Over in the corner was a box the size of a large television, wrapped in red paper and tied with a blue-and-white bow.

"Where's this from?" Duncannon asked.

"Delivered this morning," Barry said. "The return address said it came from Day."

Duncannon opened the envelope taped to the top, and his smile suddenly disappeared. "Okay, everybody. Party's over. Let's get back to work." He handed me the card, which read:

> Dear Mike Duncannon,
>
> Now that Toad Gecko is gone, *you* are the biggest asshole in the Republican Party.
>
> I thought this would suit you. Happy Birthday.
>
> Free the Fortune 500

Duncannon started to remove the gift wrap.

"Maybe you shouldn't open it," I said. "It might be dangerous."

"Harry, if you let people scare you, you're sunk."

Inside was a cardboard box tightly taped at every seam. Duncannon took a letter opener from one of the desks and began cutting his way in. As soon as he lifted the lid, a familiar sweet stench filled the room.

"Oh, shit!" I said.

"That's right, Harry."

The box contained what the experts in such things later determined was 145 pounds of fresh elephant dung. "Probably from the National Zoo," they said, which, frankly, I could have guessed myself. Stuck into it were fifty-seven candles and, right in the center, a stick of dynamite with a neatly lettered note that read: "And one for good luck."

The police and FBI weren't able to learn much. There were

46

no clues from the delivery service or the zoo. A few of Duncannon's political adversaries were on the board of the National Zoo, but no one had noticed them skulking around the elephants with buckets and shovels recently. Duncannon wrote the incident off as an isolated bit of nastiness.

The press loved it. At a time when everyone was genuinely upset about the Unabomber going after corporate types and academics, reporters found a bit of comic relief in the notion that some deranged corporate executive would have it in for Mike Duncannon. The *Post* dubbed the culprit the CEO Bomber, and the name stuck.

3

"You know, every fetus is a Republican," Duncannon said, waggling his glass of whiskey. "The unborn multitudes of our potential voters. Just think of it. Abortion is just prenatal genocide by liberals. We come into this world naturally God-fearing and conservative, and the strong stay that way while the weak turn into homosexuals and Democrats."

It was just after one in the morning. We were going over the numbers on the latest polls, trying to figure out how to appeal to everybody yet present a consistent platform and stick to our ideals. The old problem. But some of Duncannon's finest opinions grew from these late-night sessions, when the booze and ideas flowed free.

"Hell's bells, put me in office and no one will *have* to piss away all this time and money on fool campaigns. We'd just pass legislation that would make everybody do what they're supposed to do, and then government could pack up and go home. We'd keep some cops, the military, and the maintenance staff. That's all you really need."

The phone rang. Barry picked it up. "Yeah. Uh-huh. Who? Oh, sure you're the pope. And I'm Napoleon Bonaparte—"

"Holy shit!" Duncannon said, hastily putting down his drink. "Give me that telephone." He turned to me and whispered, "They said he might call, but I never thought I'd really hear from him."

Duncannon dropped to his knees and actually *crawled* to the telephone. The power of religion is amazing. I'd known it all my life, but it still surprised me to see grown men reduced to pudding by hot air, blue smoke, and incense. In moments of despair I always remembered a man could still command a lot of respect in the religion biz. It was something to fall back on. There's good money to be made.

"Yes, Your Holiness. . . . Oh, yes, Your Holiness. . . . Absolutely, Your Holiness. . . . Right away, Your Holiness."

Pope Peter Paul was breezing through Baltimore on his whirlwind North American tour. It was late for us, but he was still on Vatican time and wanted to see Mike.

It didn't matter what time it was. For Mike Duncannon, a private audience with the pope was even more important than being president. He showered, brushed his teeth, and gargled with mouthwash three times to banish every whiff of whiskey from his breath. He fretted over his wardrobe for twenty minutes—not that there was much choice—settling on a sort of undertaker outfit to demonstrate humility and respect. He even insisted that the driver go slow on the way to Baltimore, as though God really cares about U.S. speed limits.

The Mod Squad stayed behind. "Sorry, guys," Duncannon said. "But a Jew, a black man, a woman—I can't risk offending the pope. You understand."

The pontiff was staying at the Doubletree Inn. He had

wanted the Omni—better suited for the pope—but the Vatican travel service didn't book far enough in advance and almost every room in town had been snatched up by pope-watchers. As it was, they got stuck with Room 666. Seems the pope was the only one not scared to take it.

Duncannon was trembling in the elevator. I thought he would faint walking down the hall. He crossed himself and muttered a prayer before pushing the doorbell.

"Come on in, it's open!" called a voice with an Eastern European accent.

The pontiff was lying on the bed, propped up by pillows. He was wearing a white sweatsuit marked "Property of the Vatican Athletic Department" and was watching an "I Love Lucy" rerun on Nickelodeon. "Hey, guys, come in. Boy, I love American TV. If we had American cable at the Vatican I don't think I would ever get anything done." He hit the mute button but didn't turn off the set.

"Your Holiness. . . ." Duncannon said reverently.

"Hey, call me Pete," the pope said.

"Pete?"

"Yeah. Pete. It's my name. In public you can call me Your Holiness, but in here let's make it Pete. You mind if I call you Mike?"

"Ahhh, no, P-P-P . . . ah, no sir, please do." He just couldn't do it.

"Believe me, Mike, when you get elected, you'll get darn sick and tired of people calling you Mr. President all the time. It's not what it's cracked up to be."

"Uh, no, sir, P-P-P . . . no, I guess not. Uh, this is Harry Beltway, who's helping run my campaign."

The pope sat up. "Not of the Beltway Family Preachers?"

"Billy Beltway was my grandfather," I said.

"Well, I'll be. . . . It's a pleasure to meet you, son. As one professional to another, I always thought your family had a real nice act. Plays a different circuit than me but, hey, *vive la différence*."

"Thank you, sir."

Duncannon was still standing, looking a little unsteady. The pope shoved a large bowl of chips toward him and gestured at a chair.

"Have a seat and help yourself. Sorry the accommodations aren't more spacious, but this is all we could get. You'll have to come see me at the Vatican sometime and I'll give you the real papal treatment."

Duncannon perched very gingerly on the edge of a green leather desk chair and politely took two or three chips. "These are good. What are they?"

"Sour cream 'n' onion communion wafers."

Duncannon dropped the chip and turned ghastly white.

The pope laughed. "Oh, it's all right. They're not blessed. The guy who makes our regular ones is experimenting. He's thinking of starting a little sideline of secular snacks. They don't go very well with wine, but there's a six-pack over in the fridge. Help yourself if you want. We've also got Bar-B-Q and Salt 'n' Vinegar, but my personal favorite so far is Cool Ranch Style."

Standing by the wall, watching this first meeting between the future head of the Free World and the head of the Catholic church, I felt like a servant. It was hard to throw Duncannon off balance, but his upbringing proved to be too much for him. I could see he couldn't believe he was actually talking to the pope. That put him at a disadvantage.

"Hey, Mike," said the pontiff, "Do you feel like going out for a jog? I can just grab my mitre and we'll run two or three miles. I've been doing an awful lot of just sitting and standing."

Duncannon looked worried. "I'm not sure that would be such a good idea around here at two-thirty in the morning."

I could imagine the headlines: POPE AND DUNCANNON MUGGED. A riot would probably break out in Baltimore.

"Well, then, how about hitting the exercise room? Let me slip something on my feet."

Duncannon noticed the pope's white Doc Marten's, specially ordered from England. "You know, if you want some other shoes, I could ask around about getting you some nice white Nikes, white Bass Weejuns, or albino Teva sandals. Whatever you like."

"That would be very nice of you, Mike. You know, it's hard to find white shoes that don't make you look like a dork."

Pope Peter Paul could really go the distance. Mike Duncannon is in great shape for a man his age, but the pontiff soon had him puffing on the treadmill, followed by half an hour on the weight machines. I stood around like a towel boy and kept an eye on the door to make sure nobody caught on to the event.

"Hot tub?" said the pope, beginning to strip down.

Getting into a tub with the pope was like bathing in holy water. I swear Duncannon dipped his fingers in and crossed himself before gingerly testing the temperature with his foot.

"Let's talk," said the pope. He swished his hands lazily in the water, then slid down to bathe his neck. He looked the picture of a man content with the world. "I wish we had brought a couple of beers."

"I could send Harry up to get some," Duncannon said.

"No. Later. Mike, I like you. We're just two plain old working men who made good. We can talk. It will be great to have a Catholic in the White House again."

"I haven't been elected yet." Duncannon usually was not so open about his doubts.

"No, Mike, and maybe you won't be. Not this time. But you will be. I have faith."

"Thank you, Your Hol . . . uh, P-P-P-Pete." I think he expected lightning to smite him when he finally got out the name.

"And I just wanted you to know that anything I can do—anything the Church can do to help you—you know, even just behind the scenes—well, you only have to let me know."

Duncannon's face lit up like a little kid's at Christmas. "Well, of course you understand that we have separation of church and state. Some people would get upset if—"

The pope held up his hand. "I understand, Mike," he said. "Neither of us likes it, but we both understand. And I know you can't change all that as fast as you'd like. But you just let me know how I can help you. I talked to some of your old teachers, Mike, and they all said you were a fine student, a fine boy. A little prone to raise hell . . ." He laughed. "But what boy isn't? Now, you don't have any woman troubles, do you?"

"W-w-woman troubles?" choked Duncannon.

"Yeah, you know, chasing after the ladies? I hate to ask, but a political candidate should stay away from the skirts. It can backfire on you, Mike."

"Oh, no. I've never done anything like that. Just ask my wife. I'm chaste . . . a chaste husband."

"Good for you. Now you just let me know—anytime—when you need some help," said Peter Paul, emerging from the tub and grabbing a towel.

Duncannon still seemed stunned. "I-I can't thank you enough. But what can I do for you in return?" I think tears actually welled up in Duncannon's eyes, though it may just have been from the chlorine.

"Mike, I've already made it to the top. I had a little help here and there on the way, and now I'm happy to do a little favor for others."

It had been a low-key but important meeting. After the hot tub they went back to the pope's room, caught the tail end of "Newhart" and another episode of "Lucy," had a few more beers, and pigged out on chips.

We made it back to McLean around 6:30 A.M. Sherry met Duncannon at the door.

"Wait till I tell you, Petunia," he said. "I've just spent the night with the pope."

Sherry stared at him in disbelief.

"Yeah, I did. If you don't believe me, ask Harry. We talked, had a few brewskies, worked out a bit, watched some TV. You know, honey, if I didn't know he was a Polack, I'd think he was just a regular American Joe."

I don't know where Duncannon gets his stamina, but Pope Peter Paul even made *him* look like a slacker. I was dead on my feet by the time I reached home. I automatically flipped on the TV while I undressed, and there was Pope Peter Paul, zipping along in his Popemobile, strewing benedictions to the crowd, not looking the least bit like a guy who's been up exercising and drinking all night.

As for me, I fell asleep before I got my left shoe off.

After Brandy Gecko's visit, Day got to thinking. The more she thought about it, the more likely it seemed that her cousins were involved. It was just the sort of thing they would do. Just the sort of thing they had always done. "Harry," she said to me, "Brandy is right."

It seems the whole Duncannon family had spent most of its existence beating people up, getting drunk, driving cars into things, and then beating more people up. It was a tribute to Duncannon's personal charm, or maybe just a comment on the country's need for an old-fashioned, two-fisted leader, that he had gotten as far as he had in spite of his record. Mike didn't hide his past. Far from it. In his columns and on television and over dinner and in his autobiography, he just loved to boast about laying people out cold, including cops.

What the Duncannons had done in the past was one thing. That could be seen as quaint. Provide character. But if the Duncannon brothers were going around kidnapping Congressmen—well, that would make Billy Carter look like the biggest campaign asset in history.

The longer the Duncannon brothers stayed away, the more

I felt the sick conviction in my gut that they did it. Mike Duncannon thought the whole thing was hilarious.

"Boy, wouldn't Pop be proud?" he said. "He would be m-a-a-ad. But he would be proud."

The Mod Squad fanned out in search of the brothers. They called every place they could think of. Nothing. They went to visit all the old Duncannon neighborhoods, because that family never strayed too far from home. Horace got himself beat up, and Barry came pretty close. Of course, the guys who did it apologized profusely when they learned they had roughed up some of Mike Duncannon's own. Said it was nothing personal: They were just observing their ethnic tradition of pounding niggers and kikes. Horace and Barry said they understood perfectly and respected them for articulating their values so clearly and forcefully. That's what freedom of expression is really for. It was like preaching to the choir, but those guys still felt so bad that they came around campaign headquarters afterward and said they'd gladly help any way they could; if we needed anybody else beat up, they'd go right out and do it for us.

Four days after Brandy Gecko's visit the phone rang. I picked it up. "Duncannon headquarters."

"Harry? Is that you? Frank Duncannon here."

I covered the mouthpiece. "Code Yellow! Get Duncannon here *now*!" I turned back to the phone. "Hey, Frank. Yeah, it's me. Where are you?"

"Ah, me and Tim and Pat took a little trip with a friend. But he hasn't been enjoying it as much as we expected. Did you ever see the movie *Deliverance*, Harry?"

"Oh, my God, Frank, you didn't . . ."

"Harry, Harry, Harry. Who do you think we are? You're talking to a Duncannon, laddie. It was on TV last night, Harry. I just wondered if you had seen it. Good movie."

"Where are you, Frank?"

"We're just down at a little place on the Maryland shore, Harry. Our friend had been looking a little overworked and tired, so we thought some fresh air and exercise would do him good."

"What kind of exercise, Frank?"

"Well, he's done a lot of running."

"Running?" Shit, this was going to be even worse than I feared.

"Yeah, running. He's a lot faster than you would think, Harry. You'd be very impressed to see him go. He's real hard to catch. But since there's three of us, we eventually wear him out."

"What else has your friend been up to?"

"He likes to swim. It's like he's in his element. You could say he swims like a fish. Or maybe like a frog. He really seems to love it."

"Does he, now?"

"Yes, Harry, he does. No matter how far out we take him in the boat he insists that he wants to make it all the way back to shore."

"You better not have hurt him, Frank."

"Hurt him? Hurt him? We're just trying to help. He looks a whole lot better than he did before we left. He's putting on a little muscle, getting a nice tan, taking off some of that flab. I do think he might need to get new clothes to fit his trim new figure. Of course, the suit he's got on now is wrecked anyway, what with the bloodstains. . . ."

"Bloodstains?!" These Duncannons were out of their minds. I started thinking of ways to get the hell out of all this. Cover my tracks so that when the cops busted the Duncannon election team they wouldn't know I had been there.

"Calm down, Harry. We were just trying to teach him how to box. You know, the poor guy never had a pop who taught him boxing the way ours did. We felt really bad that he'd been deprived, but we thought it's never too late to learn." He paused and sighed. "I guess we were wrong, Harry. He was not a quick learner. But we kept trying. And it was a great teacher-student ratio. One that American schools could be proud of."

Why was I doing this? Why was I born? I could have done so many things with my life, and here I was, slowly losing altitude, going down in flames. And I hadn't even had the fun of a crime. I was just an accessory after the fact. Or was it a fact? Maybe it was just a bad dream. My last desperate hope.

Duncannon burst in. I could feel his vitality fill the room even before I saw him or heard the great bellow. He was grinning and laughing.

"Frank's on the phone? Great! Gimme that, Harry. Let me talk to him!"

I handed him the phone. Then I went for a walk around the block. I needed some air.

When the call from Frank came in, Peggy paged Duncannon over at the Holocaust Museum, where he was buttonholing visitors, socking them on the shoulder as usual, telling them how great he thought it was.

Horace, who was with him, was happy for the excuse to get Duncannon back to headquarters. The appearance had been a little strange.

"Work sets you free," Duncannon had been telling the sisterhood from a B'nai Brith chapter in Indiana. "Great motto—though of course better in the original German—the sort of noble sentiment that built America: people working with their muscles and brains to make a nation strong." And those walls and barbed wire, he said, were a wonderful idea—keep the foreigners out, maintain a unified community of working Jews inside. It was the sort of thing he wanted to do with America, to build up the walls and watch GATT and NAFTA go down the toilet. The Germans were lucky, he said. They had seen the future. And if there were a few flaws the first time around, well, we wouldn't keep whining about the past and waste millions of dollars figuring out what went wrong. We'd just work together to make it perfect next time.

"Damn," I said to Horace when I found out what had happened. Duncannon had gotten his facts a little mixed up again. I saw I'd have to go and do some serious spin control the next day. Then I caught myself. What was I thinking? One second I'd decided to get the hell out, and the next I was right back in the role I most detested: the Duncannon campaign Pooper Scooper.

Duncannon had gotten off the phone. "Hey, Harry." He gave me a quick jab to the shoulder, then feinted a left hook to my stomach. "Keep your guard up, Harry, my boy. Keep your guard up." He was in such a cheerful mood he couldn't keep himself from dancing lightly around as he happily pretended to beat the crap out of me. The Duncannons weren't normally dancing boxers. None of this floating butterfly nonsense. Their pop had taught them that you didn't need to move if you decked the other guy with your first shot. It was the way Mike Duncannon ran his campaign, too.

"Harry, my lad, let me buy you a couple of drinks. We've got to talk."

The Mod Squad trickled along behind him. So did a couple of popsies. And some of the guys from the neighborhood, still itching for a fight, wanting to make amends. We looked like a street gang.

There were still ninety minutes left in Happy Hour at the Capital Grille down the street, so the double whiskeys and beer chasers came two at a time.

"Did you all hear how Frank and Pat and Tim got Toad Gecko out of town?" asked the proud brother.

Oh, good Lord. I looked around. No perms in the place, but what did it matter? Somebody would talk to the press. Or to the police. He was giving evidence free to the world.

"They told him they had close ties to the movie business. It's true. A guy we went to school with owns a video store. They said they had been thinking about the possibility of his science fiction novel being turned into a movie. And that's true, too. I was there. We all said the only thing worse than that book itself was if it got made into a movie. And then they told Br'er Toad that he had the makings of a star—the look, the hair, sort of a William Devane thing. Well, he just lapped it up. Actors and singers all want to be politicians. But you know what? Politicians all want to become actors and singers."

Duncannon banged his fist on the bar and called for a round on him for everyone. He didn't need to. Everybody was already scarfing down drinks as fast as they could, except for the neighborhood guys, who were taking a short break to beat up a couple of Ted Kennedy's aides who had been minding their own business in a corner booth.

"Well, Br'er Toad deliberated for about two seconds. He had urgent business in the House, major legislation coming down, people depending on him. . . . 'The country, or me?' he asked himself. So off they went."

I couldn't sleep for the next few nights. I expected the FBI to take me away at any moment. I thought, at the very least, that the perms would be beating down our doors to find out about Gecko.

TOAD—HAVE YOU CROAKED? This was the headline in the Washington *City Paper* sitting in all the freebie boxes on my way to work. Gecko, who had always had perfect attendance in Congress, had been absent for over a month.

The Mod Squad and I stopped by the Capital Grille for a drink. Toad's failure to appear was the major topic of conversation among all the Hill types getting sloshed on vodka and pineapple, a drink the bartender had invented in honor of our arch-nemesis.

"I think he just freaked out," said a young guy from Bob Kerrey's office.

"Nah, he just found out that he really *is* Captain Kangaroo, and he needs some time to adjust," said a snide young woman working for Barney Frank.

Horace and Barry made their excuses—kids in the suburbs, et cetera. Peggy and I ordered another round of martinis, and I decided that she was one of the few people I could trust. I lowered my voice and leaned toward her. "Peggy, what do you think about the Duncannon brothers' role in Gecko's disappearance?"

"I didn't hear anything. I don't know anything about it."

I needed to talk about it. What if a member of Congress was murdered by a bunch of misguided middle-aged hoodlums?

Even though Peggy didn't want to talk about our problems at the office, we found that we had many things in common. We drank our martinis and laughed a lot. We were both "M*A*S*H" fans and knew the plots to all the episodes. After a few drinks we sang all the words to the theme song from "Welcome Back, Kotter." On the way home we shared a cab and there was no question that I wanted to go to her place. But I desperately needed to be alone and think about whether I was getting myself deep into Judas—Jody Braggart—territory.

Horace was addicted to all-talk news radio. He often sat at his desk wearing headphones, grooving to the latest Rush diatribe or listening in on local call-in shows. One day Horace gave a big whoop, tore off the phones, and began an improvised victory dance around the office. "The General has called off the troops!" he cried. "Orville Clayton declared a truce with politics. He has disarmed!"

We all breathed a sigh of relief. We no longer had to run

against an American God. From now on, it would just be us mortals.

The popsies had a way of disappearing when you needed them most, so I had trained myself to do my own copies. I was standing at the photocopy machine, trying to reduce the size of some unruly news clippings, when an entourage swept past me into Duncannon's office: a tall angular man in a well-tailored brown herringbone suit, followed by four youths in regulation blue suits with dazzling white shirts and rep ties.

"Darryl Dent," whispered Peggy, passing by on her way to fetch her fifteenth coffee of the day.

I didn't know Darryl Dent personally, but I was well acquainted with his type. Right-wing vigilantes and state militiamen were an important part of my grandfather's inner circle. They scare me. They are severely delusional. Their charisma is always way out of proportion to their actual power, and whenever they discover that their ideas are just too wacky to fly in mainstream America, they explode in anger. (And, since they all seem to be packing artillery, you don't want to be around when it happens.)

Darryl Dent was the leader of the FFF—Fu Flux Foundation—an extremist group that lately had been trying very hard to look like the Rotary Club, but it wasn't working, despite Dent's clean-cut looks and articulate personality. He was dynamite on television and successful at raising money for political campaigns. He had been well on his way to becoming a major conservative celebrity until the Big O—the Oklahoma bombing—happened. Suddenly funny paramilitary guys with bomb cellars and big gun collections weren't just amusing political kitsch; they were downright dangerous. President Clanton had gone on record as blaming the Darryl Dents of the world for creating an atmosphere of hate and contributing to senseless tragedies. It was hard to put any kind of spin on dead babies, that's for sure.

Barry Orenstein had been in the office with Duncannon. He came out and motioned to me. "Mike wants you to go in. You'll forgive me if I'm feeling a little nauseous. I'm sure you'll love meeting Mr. Dent."

"Come in, Harry, come in," Duncannon said as I entered. "Harry, meet Darryl Dent. Darryl, this is my new right-hand man, Harry Beltway."

Dent had an extra-firm handshake and a steely glint in his eye. "Yes. My parents knew your grandfather. They were mighty sorry when he passed on."

"Thank you." I stared at his shoes, which gleamed with a spit-and-polish military shine.

"Harry, I want to float something by you here," said Duncannon. "Surely you know about Darryl's constituency—fine Americans—and how important they could be to us in this race."

Dent could barely contain his anger. "Mike, skip the shit about constituencies and America. The bottom line is, you don't want to be seen with me."

"Now, Darryl, that's simply not true."

"Oh, yeah? Then why won't you put on that uniform and pose with me?" He gestured to the leather sofa, where he had laid out two FFF uniforms—brocade capes made of bed-spreads with tasseled hoods. One of the clean-cut youths was lurking at the side, camera in hand.

Duncannon sighed. "We've been over this a million times, Big D. I love you. I love what you stand for. You're a fine, honest man, but politically you're still right of Attila the Hun. You'd scare away more voters than you'd bring in, boy. I *pay* people big bucks to position me as a nonextremist. People like Barry Orenstein, who just left this office."

"The Yid?"

"Yes, Darryl. I really don't think it was necessary to ask him if that was cream cheese and lox on his Rasputin beard."

Dent laughed. "Okay, so you won't pose with the uniform on. I can understand. You don't want to favor one organization. So let Fred here just take a shot of the two of us together, real casual, in civvies."

Duncannon looked dubious. "Harry, what do you think?"

"Sure, if you want to lynch yourself," I said, knowing how much that particular verb would irritate Dent. "I wouldn't advise it. Remember what happened to Lumpy Pruitt."

Dent pounded his fist on the table. "Goddammit, Mike. You were a pussy about that. Lumpy didn't do anything wrong, just spoke to a couple of groups that wanted to hear about you and your candidacy."

"Paramilitary groups," I said quietly.

"Did I fire Lumpy?" Mike demanded. "No, I didn't."

"But you sure as hell didn't come out and say he was right, either," said Dent.

"I never fired him," insisted Mike. "Lumpy Pruitt left because he knew that the press would be all over that thing for months. He wants to see me become president and put into action all the things he's always fought for. I love Lumpy. Had him and his wife out to the house only last week."

I made a tactical decision. "Mr. Duncannon, I'm sorry, but we've got to leave for that meeting, remember?"

"Huh?" said Mike, taking a second to respond. "Oh, yeah. That meeting. It's been nice, Darryl. Stop in again sometime." Before Darryl could say anything, I whisked Duncannon out of the office and toward the door. Dent's henchmen were still packing up the brocade capes and photo equipment. I waved to Horace as we passed his desk. Horace had a new sign, "Mr. Jitterbug, Senior Negro," taped up on his computer monitor.

Horace sprang to his feet. "Mr. Dent, Mr. Dent! Get out those robes. Don't put that camera away. I'd love to have my picture taken with you!"

About two weeks after my phone conversation with Frank Duncannon, a small package arrived at headquarters via UPS. It contained a frog's leg, a videocassette, and a note:

> Dear Folks,
>
> We thought of sending this tape to the media to awaken America to the foreign threat. What do you think?
>
> Frank

The tape showed Toad Gecko, clad only in his BVDs, fastened to a wooden chair with duct tape. Around him stood three Arabs, or rather, three large Scotch-Irish guys dressed for a toga party with Holiday Inn towels draped around their heads, and with the trademark Duncannon cordovans poking out from the bottoms of their sheets.

"America, we have Toad Gecko," the tallest one, Frank,

screeched in some weird, generic foreign accent. "We are sending you one of his legs. If you do not give us six atomic bombs so that we can blow up people we hate, we will send you Toad Gecko's other leg."

"Why would we want Toad Gecko's leg?" Day asked disgustedly. "Let him keep it."

"I like it," Duncannon said. "It has a ring of authenticity."

They both laughed and played the tape back half a dozen times. I was never quite sure just how seriously to take this family.

I had some rough patches during those weeks. Sometimes I didn't sleep nights, and I thought seriously about quitting the campaign. Yet things kept coming up. We were traveling almost constantly, and somehow I felt safer when I was away from Washington. I would forget all about Gecko and spin and numbers and just enjoy watching Mike feasting on America.

One day, as we approached Hanover, New Hampshire, Mike called to the driver, "Pull into this mall, willya? My belly's starting to growl. I've gotta put some fuel in the old furnace." He nudged me in the side. "And we'll press a little flesh and sock a few arms. It always gives the people a thrill when a candidate turns up where he's not expected."

We arrived at the mall's food court to find none other than President Jeb Clanton standing in line in front of us at the rib stand.

"Hey, Mr. President, how's it going? How are the kids?" Duncannon boomed.

Clanton glared. "How are yours?"

Mike glared back. "What are you doing up here? Feeling a little uncertain about getting your party nomination?"

"Naw, Mike, just passing through, and I thought I'd stop and cheer you fellows up. Set a little example for you, maybe, show that you, too, could be president of the United States one day, when you grow up."

"So how's the food, Mr. President?"

"Well, I don't think anyone comes to New Hampshire for the ribs, but they've got to be better than the Italian food I just had over on the other side of the food court. By the way, have you seen your colleagues yet?"

Claude Locke sat at a little table with his campaign manager. He had finished an Egg McMuffin, a bag full of Chicken McNuggets, and a large mound of french fries. His handler was trying to persuade him to save a Quarter Pounder with cheese until later, but Claude would have none of it. He waved it at us gaily and began feeding it into his mouth.

"Pineapple's here, too," said Clanton. "He was wandering around, couldn't figure out what he wanted, but I guess he finally found something."

There he was in the corner, eating vanilla frozen yogurt in a cup. "This is very good ice cream," he said to us. "Soothing. Well, actually it's not really ice cream, it's yogurt, but it tastes the same and is much healthier for you. Or at least so they tell me. And Bill Pineapple has no reason to disbelieve them. It seems perfectly sensible to me. So it's quite good. You should try some. If you like that sort of thing, and if you're hungry right now."

Well, Mike Duncannon did try some. He tried the vanilla

and the chocolate. He didn't like the stuff very much, but then he went on to try the strawberry and a whole bunch of other flavors, with as many toppings as he could squeeze on. And that was just his appetizer before making the rounds, one by one, of every damn food stand in that court—deli, Chinese, Greek, hamburgers, ribs, pizza, more burgers, hot dogs, fries, salad bar, gourmet cookies—you name it. And at every single stop he was shaking hands and punching shoulders until you wondered whether there would be a man left in New Hampshire who could raise his right arm the next day without wincing in memory of his meeting with Mike Duncannon.

They went for it. I had been spending so much time in the campaign offices recently, fighting fires and wrenching strategy out of thin air, that I had forgotten how he thrived on the PEOPLE. He just loved touching them and feeling them and grinning his big old Scotch-Irish grin at them and asking them how they were and what they did and how the wife and kids and house and car and jobs and everything else were. And every single one of them, without exception, went away feeling that Mike Duncannon had talked to them alone, that he truly knew and cared about them.

4

What was Mike Duncannon doing, wowing the people of New Hampshire? On paper it didn't make any sense: a Washington Catholic waving the Confederate flag and pulling in votes from a bunch of hatchet-faced Yankees. But in your gut it was sublimely reasonable. They all distrusted big government and outsiders, and Mike Duncannon always seemed, even the first time you met him, to be just folks, somebody you had always known, someone who wouldn't think twice before rolling up his shirtsleeves and helping change your tire or raise your barn or reopen that factory or make our nation great again.

And Mike Duncannon threw snowballs, which was something Bill Pineapple wouldn't do and possibly had never done in his life. Mike even had good aim. He knocked Orson Kane's brand-new L.L. Bean hat right off his head with the very first shot, and he and two of his brothers, Pat and Joseph, already had him down on the ground with his face in a pile of snow, just like the good old days, when Day pulled them off and reminded them that playfulness is good press, but it looks bad if you actually make another candidate cry.

They loved him up there in the North Country, warts and all. They didn't seem to care that the press had exposed two card-carrying bigots in his organization during the past week alone. He was one of them. When he put on his rubbers, like a good Catholic schoolboy, and went out shoveling sidewalks in Littleton after the blizzard, just to help people out and, as he said, to earn a few honest quarters to fund his campaign, the townspeople flocked to him. Little old ladies cashed their Social Security checks and paid him $100 for clearing off their front steps.

"Hiya, Harry, how's everything?" the voice said over the telephone. A shiver ran down my spine. It was Randy Tate, Pineapple's research director, or master of dirty tricks. He wouldn't dream of being so polite unless he had scored some major embarrassing triumph. Randy and I had attended Pigeon Forge Military Academy together, and even back then he had been a snitch and a creep. He reported me for smoking pot in the latrine, and I spent four weeks scrubbing down hallways. Randy was pissed because he had expected me to be expelled, but he hadn't counted on the Billy Beltway factor. Those Jesus dollars come in handy sometimes.

I tried to act cool. "Well, Randy, we're having a little problem here," I said.

"Oh, I'm sorry to hear that, Harry. Anything I can do to help?"

"Maybe there is. We can't decide between gold or red curtains for the Oval Office. What do you think?"

"Well, I don't think you need to worry about that at all. I

just called to say you might want to turn on Channel 5 and have a look at our new ad. It's kind of a nice spot, I think. I thought of it myself."

Oh, shit! I bantered with him for about another twelve seconds, not wanting to let on I was worried. Then I ran into the other room where Day and our candidate were talking. "Turn on the TV! Major emergency!"

It was worse than I thought. The spot opened with a nice, flattering shot of Mike during the New Hampshire speech, knocking 'em dead with the stuff about no more sellouts and bringing jobs home to America. Then they freeze-framed him in the middle of the word "America" and a voice-over said, "America comes out of Mike Duncannon's mouth, but his ears are full of Japan." Cut to a fuzzy shot of Duncannon in some electronics store buying a tape recorder. "I'll take the Sony," he said. "You can't beat 'em for quality."

"Dammit!" Day shouted. A Coke bottle flew across the room and shattered high on the wall. "Dammit! Where the fuck did they get that?"

"They must have been following me, the bastards," said Duncannon.

The ad went on. "And his belly's full of France. . . ." A shot of him entering Provence, one of his favorite restaurants, with this shit-eating grin of anticipation on his face . . .

". . . and China . . ." Leaving Asia Nora, the most effete Eastern eatery in D.C., laughing uproariously . . .

". . . and MEXICO!" Mike at Mixtec with salsa dripping down his chin and a Corona in his hand . . .

A glass went right through the television screen this time. I didn't even get to hear the punchline. Day didn't care.

"Mike, give me the keys to your house!" she ordered.

"What? What?" Mike muttered, still dazed by the Pineapple coup.

"Keys. NOW!" He handed them over. "Harry, come with me!"

"Where are we going?"

"We're going to do a little housecleaning."

We drove, in her American car, at top speed over to Mike's house. Sherry cowered in a corner as Day rampaged through room by room, pulling off the shelves and out of closets and drawers everything she could find that was not made in the USA. "Maybe we should have stopped and rented a U-Haul," she said. The television, gone. Half of the kitchen appliances, almost all of the plates and cutlery, gone. "He's going to need to buy himself some new clothes, I'm afraid. I don't think six pairs of underpants and three shirts will get him very far."

"So what are we going to do with all this stuff, Day?" I asked after about an hour. Sherry had barricaded herself upstairs in the master bathroom amid her Lancôme and Chanel bottles. Foreign junk was piled waist deep in the hall. Tools and sporting goods spilled out the front door and down the steps.

"We are going to call a press conference, and in front of the cameras we are going to have the biggest damn bonfire you ever saw."

Sherry's sadness about the sacking of her house soon gave way to pure joy when she realized that her job for the next few weeks would be to shop, shop, shop. By the time we set out for

Texas, Sherry had a beautiful new wardrobe of top American-designed suits.

We were going to the Lone Star State to attend one of those generic, spectacular GOP fund-raisers, organized by the ladies in their tennis whites from the affluent suburbs of Houston. And boy, had they organized! They'd even managed to get celebrities from Los Angeles and New York there for the day. The scuttlebutt was that the party appeared to be fragmented and headed for disaster in the fall, so this event was supposed to show our solidarity and be bipolar, not bipartisan. Conservatives and moderates together, and even some independent types. Gerald Ford came down from Michigan and clowned for the crowd in his golfing clothes. Arnold was there with Maria, and Brooke brought along Andre. Clint made an appearance along with his orangutan co-star of long ago, Clyde, who was visiting for the day from the petting zoo he'd retired to over near Austin. All eyes turned when Princess Di strolled in wearing a hat that was worthy of the Ascot races.

I felt sorry for poor Pineapple—the highlight of the day was the Celebrity Candidate Tennis Match, and he just didn't have the strength to play with his bum arm. He looked even more pathetic than usual, dressed in tennis shorts, sneakers, and a white LaCoste shirt. He even held a white pen in his right hand. "Bill Pineapple is not old," I heard him telling a group of perms in the reception area of the clubhouse. "Bill Pineapple just ran up and down these stairs thirty times! Bill Pineapple is a war hero. That is why he cannot play tennis. Bill Pineapple sacrificed his biceps for his country."

Lemuel Atwater came bounding out of the locker room,

trying to attract some perm attention. His nerd-jock look included baggy, knee-length knit shorts and a new version of his ubiquitous flannel shirt of white and khaki plaid. His outfit worked wonders. Leroy Turner, the reporter from the *New Republic* who had done the most to make Lemuel's shirt a cause célèbre, came running over. "Governor, *nice shirt*. But it's not all white. Are they going to let you play?"

"The shirt stays," said Lemuel, with more forcefulness than he usually displayed on major issues.

Our man emerged. I have to say, Sherry had dressed him perfectly. No frou-frou European tennis duds, just nice, All-American Brooks Brothers tennis whites, with one of those white cotton sweaters trimmed in red, white, and blue casually tied around his neck. "Well, boys, it *is* how you play the game. We're gonna whup 'em today, and whup 'em at the polls."

Fred Tisch from the *New York Times* stepped forward and threw the bombshell: "Mr. Duncannon, we've come across some information showing that you keep a regular room at the Willard Hotel, and that you visit someone in that room every Tuesday and Thursday afternoon. Any comments?"

Duncannon turned whiter than his outfit. I started to usher him away. "We have no comment," I said. "We're here to play some tennis and raise some money." Fortunately, just as the reporters started following us onto the tennis courts, a great ruckus ensued at the main entrance.

"You cannot throw me out! I am here to play. I am a contender! You cannot exclude me from the party!" It was Claude Locke, looking enormous and even blacker than ever in his 48-waist tennis shorts and long, flipperlike sneakers.

"I'm sorry, sir. You're not on our official guest list," said the security guard patiently as his underlings restrained Locke.

"Yes, I know. I'm not a guest—I AM A CANDIDATE!"

"Please, sir, I'm going to have to ask you to leave. Please don't make me call the police."

"I BELIEVE IN AMERICA! THE STREETS NEED TO BE SAFE. I NEED TO PLAY TENNIS! YOUNG GIRLS ARE HAVING BABIES! I NEED TO PLAY TENNIS!"

The perms were on it in a second. "Mr. Locke, Mr. Locke," they all shouted, hoping to grab a sound bite from Claude, who at this point was nearly foaming at the mouth.

"Mr. Locke, you're wearing tennis whites, and yet you are not white, and you were not invited to this fund-raiser. Is this a racial thing?"

"Huh?" grunted Locke as the cops arrived and handcuffed him. By now, Duncannon had slipped away unnoticed, yet I stood there, fascinated at the spectacle of a candidate being led away in cuffs. The cops shoved his head down so that he got into the car without mishap, but they closed the door on his foot. They opened and closed it again from the inside as the car sped away and Locke's campaign manager, a nice young black Dartmouth graduate, went running after it around the country club's circular driveway.

I recovered and went to see how my athlete was doing. One look and I knew he was pissed. And when a Duncannon is pissed, he beats up on somebody—anybody who's available. This time it was the unfortunate Lemuel Atwater. Duncannon was spiking his shots over the net to anywhere Lemuel wasn't. His hearty, brutal Scotch-Irish serves were beating the shit out of Lemuel, who was clearly accustomed to playing a friendly round of doubles with his wife and the neighbors. Mike was like a machine—he kept 'em coming and didn't even seem to have to catch his breath. Great streams of sweat began cascading down Lemuel's head from the tip of his cowlick down to his little dimpled chin. One of his popsies minced out to hand him a sweatband—plaid flannel, of course—and as he weakly bent his head down to receive it, I recognized the signs.

Lemuel looked just like the Old Elephant King in Babar right after he ate the bad mushroom, or Jimmy Carter just before he collapsed while jogging, or Gordy Hedge when he was about to blow his breakfast in Tokyo. I knew it was only a matter of minutes, and I was right. Three more serves, and Lem sank to the ground in a pained, plaid stupor. His aides rushed out to try to help him. He looked up into their faces, unable to speak, his lips writhing, his teeth gnashing.

It was not Mike Duncannon's finest hour. Lemuel Atwater had suffered a stroke, and many people who were watching believed it had been Duncannon's fault. He didn't make it any easier, either, in his comments to the press. "I told him to take off that damn fool flannel shirt of his. It's just heatstroke, plain and simple."

But it wasn't heatstroke, it was the real thing. Atwater lay semiconscious in the intensive care unit of Houston's best hospital. Bill Pineapple went there immediately—the news at five showed him carrying a huge floral arrangement with a big plaid bow. Orson Kane sent his own plane to New York to fly down five top neurologists. The trillionaire then announced that he would no longer campaign "until my good friend Lemuel is back on his feet." Kane's numbers went up three points. Even Claude Locke got a cute sound bite out of it: "Gee, I'm in mighty rotten shape, too, and maybe if I had been allowed to play, I would have been matched against the governor. He would have had an easier time."

And what did our boy Mike do? Brag. The news showed him demonstrating his vicious backhand and reliving all his greatest shots against Atwater. "If you can't take the heat, get out of the kitchen," he told reporters as he vowed to keep campaigning. Naturally, the papers murdered us the next day. Plus, "Willardgate," as the perms had dubbed it, was building up steam. The *Washington Post* reproduced hotel receipts for the last six months showing how often Duncannon had stayed there. The *New York Post* was more direct: HAS MR. RIGHT BEEN MESSING AROUND WITH MISS WRONG?

What *was* this hotel stuff about? I feared the worst. My experience around evangelical types had shown that when sex reared its ugly head, it was more hideous than you could imagine. I dreaded talking to Duncannon and spent days replaying in my head the scene with Judas that had made me leave his employ. "Okay, so a twelve-year-old-girl. Yeah, they got pictures. So what?" Judas had said the week the *National Enquirer* blew the lid on his sordid hobbies. I left shortly thereafter and soon found my way to Africa. Praise Jesus.

I decided to get all of Mike's closest advisers together and confront him in a comfortable setting. I wanted Sherry to be there. She should know what we were in for, and maybe her reaction would help us decide if we should continue the race. I called and set up a meeting at the Duncannons' Barbed

Palace in McLean for eight o'clock in the evening, two days after Lemuel's stroke. The Mod Squad, Sam Magillicuddy, and I arrived in the campaign van. Sherry greeted us at the door in a frilly apron with a tray of cheese-puff canapés. Day stood behind her, looking tense.

"You poor dears, you've been working so hard," Sherry cooed. "Come in. I've fixed martinis. Day's got a head start on the drinks, so why don't you all grab one or two and start catching up? Mike will be right down."

We were halfway through our perfectly stirred concoctions when Mike arrived, resplendent in a green paisley smoking jacket. "What's up, kids? Why the secrecy?"

I cleared my throat. This was going to be hard. "I've taken the liberty of preparing a packet of information for everyone," I said, passing around folders. "You can refer to them as I'm speaking.

"Now, sir, and Mrs. Duncannon, we've got a delicate situation on our hands. It's this hotel thing. The perms have dug up receipts, and now 'Hard Copy' claims to have gotten hold of some footage of a mysterious blonde, wrapped up in scarves, leaving a room where they say Mr. Duncannon stays in the afternoons." I stopped and looked over at Sherry, who was shaking and turning purple. "I'm sorry. I know this is hard, Mrs. Duncannon, but we've got to get to the bottom of this and then figure out what to do. It could easily be a turning point in this campaign."

A strange guttural sound escaped Sherry's lips. Duncannon rushed over to his wife, who then began, violently, uncontrollably, to *laugh*.

79

"Petunia," said Duncannon, giggling. "Hold steady, there, girl, we sure got 'em going." He reached into his breast pocket and offered her his handkerchief. She dabbed her eyes as she continued to shake with high-pitched squeals of laughter.

Day had had it. "Okay, you two, enough with the private joke. Would you like to *share* now?"

"Honey?" squealed Sherry, appealing to Mike.

"Well . . . Sherry and I get together every Tuesday and Thursday afternoon. Watch movies. It was her idea, read about it in one of her darn fool women's magazines or something. But it's nice, I gotta admit. You know how I love movies."

"So the mysterious blonde is you?" I asked Sherry.

" 'Keep Your Love Alive,' that was the title of the article," she explained. "I think it was in *Christian Woman.* Lots of good ideas, like wrapping yourself up naked in Saran Wrap—"

"You're fresh enough, my dear. Please don't do that!" Duncannon cut in.

"—and one of the ideas was to rent a hotel room once in a while, just the two of you, and kind of snuggle and watch videotapes."

"Yes, snuggle," repeated Duncannon. "We were only watching videotapes. It's just that the Willard is a few blocks from the office, and we thought it would be a fun idea to meet during the day."

"Sir," I said, embarrassed. "You don't have to explain anything you do with your own wife. I mean, you're consenting adults."

Duncannon suddenly grabbed the collar of my shirt. "WE WERE ONLY WATCHING—NOTHING ELSE, GET IT?"

"Yes, nothing else," echoed Sherry in a sad, meek tone, all of her joviality suddenly drained.

Between the Atwater incident and Willardgate, Duncannon's image was taking a beating. Our popularity had dropped by about ten points, and everyone was saying we should get out of the race so that Bill Pineapple could unify the party. *Newsweek* ran a cover with a close-up of Duncannon screaming, his fist in the air. The headline read, SPOILSPORT! I thought we were goners until Duncannon pulled his Video Rewind move.

"Call a press conference," he said. "I'm pretty miffed about all these reporters trailing around after me and my wife." He was wrong about the reporters—hardly anyone was following us at all. But we pulled in as many perms as we could.

We staged the thing in a small video store in Waco and provided popcorn. The candidate was charming, Siskel and Ebert all rolled into one and seasoned with a dash of Michael Medved for conservative flavor. One of the male popsies, Stuart, had produced a montage of the Duncannons' favorite videos. Another volunteer, Marcia, had prepared handouts listing their favorite movies, each rated with up to four little American flags for "must watch."

His speech was pure FV—Family Values. He held up the pictures of Sherry at the hotel. "That's no lady, that's my wife," he bellowed. Then he explained how wholesome their movie trysts had been. He waxed eloquent about how quintessentially American the movies were. After all, they were invented by one of the greatest Americans who ever lived, Thomas Alva Edison. He talked Bogart and Cagney. He talked

Capra. He talked Eastwood and Schwarzenegger and Babe (the porcine one, not the baseball player). He quoted *The Lou Gehrig Story* and, to show his multicultural diversity, *To Kill a Mockingbird*.

In show biz parlance, he killed, and it made all the difference for us. Overnight, he went from being philandering Mike the spoilsport to Movie Mike, the doting husband of every housewife's dreams. *Entertainment Weekly* made us its cover story. Mike's movie list was picked up by all the wire services. Blockbuster video stores announced that they would have a special "Mike Section" at the front of every store featuring good, clean American films. Finally, in a really inspired move, Duncannon flew to Houston to present the now-recovering Lemuel Atwater with his own personal collection of favorite videotapes along with a case of microwavable popcorn. Photos of the Atwaters and Duncannons were in every paper the next day.

Pineapple was furious. He called Day. "We should get together and talk about how we're splitting the party apart," he whined.

"We have no intention of talking about anything," said Day.

"Why? Is your cousin too busy watching movies? You know, Bill Pineapple watches movies. He watches plenty of movies."

Day hung up.

Over the last few tough weeks, Peggy and I had been thrown together often. I found myself thinking about her more and more whenever I returned to the drab studio apartment I had rented in Foggy Bottom. She was a hiker, it turned out, and in our brief spells of spare time, we began taking walks along the C&O canal together and occasionally shared cooking chores at her place or mine. We didn't know if the friendship would ever veer toward romance—we were just enjoying each other's company and taking what came.

One night we were hanging around in my apartment listening to some Joan Osborne tapes. She was cooking tofu with spinach when the phone rang. I answered it.

"You really believe he's not boinking some bimbo in that hotel room?" said the voice on the other end.

"Hi, Dad. Nice hearing your voice." It had been over two years since I'd talked to my father, but he had sent pictures of his latest wedding, held this time on the veranda of his house in Guadalajara. I had shuddered involuntarily then upon seeing his gray ponytail trailing down the back of his white Cuban shirt, and I shuddered now to think of him giving anyone political advice.

"They're always boinking 'em, kid. It's the first rule of politics and religion. Remember Grandpa and his bevy of Christian cuties?"

"I sure do."

"Your poor grandmother. I hope she's resting in peace, but as far away from Jesus as possible." There was a painful pause. My father was always trying to get me to turn against my evangelical past. He continued. "Well, then, Harry, I'm sure you can guess what Brother Duncannon is doing in that hotel room. Come home and stop working for assholes. Sierra and I have plenty of room for you down here. You need a break, and Africa wasn't it."

"Dad. He's not an asshole. He and his wife are decent people, and I'm proud to work on their campaign. It's the first time I've believed in something and not been disappointed."

"Well, you're going to be. How can you believe that he's really watching videos with his wife? He's acting like he's still in high school dreaming up excuses for his parents. You watch. He'll be caught with his pants down, I guarantee it."

After I had gotten off the phone and punched a few walls, Peggy handed me a plate of perfectly cooked tofu. "Parents can be a real pain in the butt," she said, flipping back her hair.

"Umm, healthy," I said, tasting my first bite.

"What's the matter with healthy? The crap we eat when we're on the road turns me into a plastic, grease-oozing organism."

"I'm not complaining. I just wouldn't think of it as good ol' American cuisine. I mean, do you think Mike Duncannon would be caught dead eating this stuff?"

"Mike Duncannon, Mike Duncannon! Don't you ever stop thinking about him? Just because I work for the guy doesn't mean I have to eat like him." Peggy looked as mad as I had after getting off the phone with Dad.

I tried to make a save. "Yeah, you're right. You know, for all his talk about America, he sure eats out in fancy places. I've never gone out to eat so much in my life. Must have gained eight pounds since I started working for him. The Jockey Club two nights a week, Provence, Jean Louis—all those rich sauces. How did a humble guy like him get such rich tastes?"

"Humble—hah!" said Peggy, glaring at me.

I lifted a big forkful of tofu and spinach and savored my

next bite. "Mmm. This is really good. I feel strong." I slurped at the spinach. "I feel like Popeye."

"So," she said, after we had finished our meal and had been staring at our plates for a few minutes, "do you want to talk about it?"

"What?"

"Your dad. What he said."

"No, because I know it's not true. He's just trying to needle me. No self-respecting liberal fuck-up on his twenty-fifth career as an importer of piñatas wants to admit that he has a son who's gaining ground in conservative political circles."

Peggy looked thoughtful. "You know, I've been meaning to ask you about your childhood. I grew up on the Upper West Side of Manhattan, so I can only imagine it. So rural, so religious. Did you go around in long white robes and throw yourself into pools of water?"

"Oh, no. My grandparents taught me how to walk *on top* of the water when I was two."

"Sorry. I just think it must have been weird, being raised by Billy Beltway."

"Well, it was and it wasn't. Like being in any other family business, I guess. It certainly turned out to be lucrative. Of course, I also still believe in our products: God, love."

"Love," repeated Peggy thoughtfully. And then like someone standing at the end of a cold pool who suddenly decides to take the plunge, she leaned across our empty plates and gave me a lingering kiss. She slid her arms around my neck. "Harry, I can't tell you how much our relationship means to me. I don't know where it's going. . . ."

At that moment I knew just where I wanted it to go. I slipped my hand under the table and rested it on her knee. She flinched.

"I'm sorry," I said. "I misunderstood."

"No, no, it's not that. But do you mind doing it my way? I get a little scared when things get out of control."

She kissed me again, longer, harder. She took my hand and led me to the couch. I liked things done her way. I liked them a lot. Control was not an issue with me.

Soon I was lying naked from the waist down on my braided living room rug with C-SPAN babbling in the background. Even though I was exhausted, I tried to be polite and asked if I could make love to her.

"Oh, it's the nineties," she explained as she inched away from me slightly across the rug. "I don't do that kind of thing anymore."

Mike Duncannon was on the road from then on constantly. It was grueling, it was exhilarating. In early March Lemuel Atwater threw in the towel—a plaid one, of course—saying that his stroke had taught him the importance of spending more time with his family. Photos showed him being wheeled out of a rehabilitation center with his three-year-old grandson on his lap. Atwater endorsed Pineapple, who went to see him the first day he was home and coached him on how to hold a pen in his weak hand to keep people from shaking it. The pen he gave him, of course, said "Pineapple for President."

So the only ones left were Pineapple, Orson Kane, and our man Mike.

The CEO Bomber had not disappeared. He had gone on-line. One morning the popsies arrived at headquarters to find that the files on their computers had been scrambled. A new screen-saver showed an animated cartoon of Mike Duncannon skipping merrily along singing:

I hate niggers,
I hate Jews,
I hate foreigners,
I hate youse.
I hate NAFTA
I hate GATT
Mike Duncannon's
Where it's at.

At that point, a Monty Pythonesque giant pineapple dropped from above, crushing the Duncannon figure flat. Then the words "Free the Fortune 500" began scrolling lazily across the screen. After about five seconds, one of those old, round, black cartoon bombs with a fuse appeared. *Fizzle. Bang!*

It took two days to sort things out again, and we brought in some techno-consultant to beef up security on the system.

I could have written off the first time as a prank, but the latest incident bore the earmark of something more serious. Everyone was on edge, and everyone was suspect. Day was convinced it was some corporate type, and started pulling strings as only she knew how. She spent a lot of her time trying to identify the culprit. Barry, who had a slight paranoid tendency anyway, thought someone in our own organization might be responsible. He ordered background checks on all the popsies, which did not exactly help morale.

Then, a week later, someone tampered with the address list file that went to the mailing house. An entire run of Duncannon fliers were automatically sent out—not to the middle-class constituents we were trying to sway, but to Mike Duncannon himself and his campaign staff. Two mail sacks of fliers waited for me at my apartment building one evening. It took three mail trucks to make the Duncannons' delivery.

Day's investigations did not unearth the culprit, but she learned that hundreds of upper level executives from multinational corporations were contributing to a charitable "CEO Bomber Defense Fund" to hire lawyers and to provide the necessary luxuries of life for the culprit, should he ever be caught. One of the nation's leading investment firms was administering the fund on a pro bono basis, and the Bomber's portfolio was already valued in excess of $47 million.

Sherry traveled a lot with Mike, but on those occasions when she was left behind, she tended to make a nuisance of herself around the office. On the road I got a call from Horace one day: "Harry, she's making me needlepoint pillows for my back, for Chrissakes. And we can't eat any more brownies. We're brownied out. Get that gal something to do."

As luck would have it, *Christian Woman,* the magazine from which Sherry had culled her video-watching tips, called the next day requesting an interview for a cover story. "It's a definite cover, right?" I said. "Not something you're going to pull if we stop winning delegates? I mean, we're not going to end up in some small column on the back page, are we?"

"Oh, certainly not," said Trish Darby, the editor. "We are very impressed with Mrs. Duncannon. Our readers will love her. We believe in her values. She's our cover girl for June, no matter what happens in the next few months."

I set up the session for early the following week and flew back from Oklahoma to personally supervise the interview and photo shoot. When I arrived, the plant rental people were arranging the last pots of geraniums in the big greenhouse off the side of the Duncannon dwelling, where the light was best for taking pictures.

"Harry, I'm so glad to see you!" Sherry gathered me up in her arms and planted a wet kiss on half my mouth. Oddly, it seemed rather arousing.

"Oh, I'm so nervous," she stammered. "What if I say something stupid?"

"Just be yourself," I said, and suddenly she grabbed my hand and placed it directly between her round, firm breasts.

"Feel my heart thumping?" gushed Sherry. "Harry Beltway, I don't know what I would do without you. Thanks ever so much for flying halfway across the country just to be my Rock of Gibraltar."

"No problem. Here's the briefing notes." I reached into my briefcase and handed her a list of issues and possible comments Peggy had prepared. "Now, just remember—this is a friendly interview and a friendly audience. They'll want to know all about you, Sherry Duncannon, the woman behind the man."

The interview went great. Sherry was girlishly charming, talking about her childhood as the only daughter of a prominent dermatologist in a small town in Michigan. She talked about how she had first met her husband on the Nixon campaign, and how he had swept her off her feet.

"So you never worked after you were married?" asked Trish Darby. (I was impressed that the head honcho editor herself was doing the interview.)

"Well, sure I did, honey, like we all do," smiled Sherry. "I worked for my man. I honestly believe that behind every great man is a great woman. I like that. It's not that he's greater, it's just that he comes first, and then he shares everything he gets." (Way to go, Sherry.)

"Any regrets that there are no children?"

Sherry's eyes began to tear. "No," she said. "No. You know, Mike's like a child himself. He's enough . . ." She tried to smile, but she was crying too hard. "Oh, Harry," she said. I was sitting in a straight chair by the living room wall. She got up, ran to me, and buried her face in my chest. "Oh, Harry."

"I'm sorry. I'm afraid Mrs. Duncannon is a little upset," I told Trish. "Could we take a brief break?"

Sherry raised her head from my chest. "At least there's Timmy," she said with a sob.

"Timmy? Who's Timmy?" Trish Darby had already scribbled the name in her notebook.

Sherry looked stricken. "Timmy. You know. My . . . dog."

Timmy—a dog? That evening at the Jockey Club her husband had said Timmy was a cat. This was getting weird. Who was the mysterious Timmy, and why had I never encountered him?

Sherry didn't regain her composure. I sent her upstairs to bed, and after about a half hour I told Trish Darby that Mrs.

Duncannon had been overextending herself and seemed to have come down with the flu. She asked if they could at least take pictures of Timmy the Dog while the afternoon light was still good, and I explained that Timmy was off at the St. Francis Puppy Seminary, a new type of boarding school for Catholic canines. I asked if they could possibly stay in town another night and come back to continue the interview the next day. To my surprise, she agreed.

After packing Trish and her photo crew into their rented van, I felt at loose ends. None of the Duncannons' three part-time servants seemed to be around. I didn't want to leave Sherry all alone, yet I didn't want to intrude on her privacy. Finally, I climbed the grand staircase and began searching for the master bedroom. I turned down the hallway at my right and saw a door ajar. A bright light was burning and I could hear tinkly music inside.

I gingerly pushed the door open and surveyed the room. It was a nursery done in European style with expensive, severe furniture and sumptuous lace linens—no IKEA here. Over the crib hung a trendy white-and-black mobile with letters hanging down, letters that spelled TIMMY. In the corner sat Sherry, rocking away in a platform rocker, holding a lifelike, hairless doll to her breast.

"So now you know," she said quietly.

"What's there to know?"

"The extent of our dysfunctional family. Isn't that what those liberals call it nowadays?" She turned the doll away from her breast to show me his ugly newborn vinyl mug. "Timmy, this is Harry, your daddy's adviser. He's going to make us win, IF no one finds out about YOU."

"Oh, Sherry," I said, and now it was time for me to start crying. There was something so beautiful, so vulnerable about her sitting there, nursing her faux baby and showing it to me. I wanted her. I wanted her bad.

"Timmy, you have to go to bed now, honey. Mommy has an important meeting," said Sherry, dropping the doll unceremoniously into its crib and stepping toward me. She led me down the hall into a girlish dressing room with a frilly daybed. She seemed to be undressed even before we had shut the door, and we fell onto the lace like gods falling onto clouds.

The ferocity of her lovemaking astounded me. As a lover, she was like every cliché in the book: an unquenchable thirst, a rising volcano, a bucking horse, a cat in heat. What can I say? For those three hours, she was my First Lady. She had my vote.

"I knew it wasn't right," she said, lighting up a Virginia Slim she fished from a sewing cabinet next to the daybed, where we lay in a tangled, satisfied mess. "On our wedding night, he told me he couldn't make love to me, that I was too nice. I waited for him to change his mind all that week, while we were on our honeymoon at Disney World, but it never happened. It's not that it's *never* happened for me. I had a couple of boyfriends before I met Mike, and I let them get to second or third base."

Sherry paused and took a drag. "Some of them even slid into home. For the first few years of our marriage, I tried everything to get him to make me feel more like a woman. I begged and he balked. I talked to Father O'Leary, who said, 'I'm sorry, little lady. I can't help you there. Mike is a nice boy. You should be happy.' I finally had to accept that Mike Duncannon would *never* make love to me."

I whistled softly. "Never, at all?" I said. "So you two really *were* just watching videos at the hotel, huh?"

"Yeah. Although not for lack of trying. I tried to slip in a porno video once. Now I live in dread fear that one of the perms, as you call them, will dig up our computer record and find out about it. Mike was furious when he saw it in my satchel. Oh, Harry."

"Yes?"

"Harry. I hope you don't think it's because I just needed someone, anyone. Harry, I've been infatuated with you. I think about you all the time. I dreamed about today, only I can't believe it really happened."

"It happened," I said, pulling her closer.

"Oh, Harry," said Mrs. Duncannon.

5

Incredibly, we had won New Hampshire. We were the lead story, the big buzz. The perms acted like we were a fluke, an overnight success.

But I knew different. I had been a witness to history, and I was hooked. I had watched us dig the votes up, one by one, like all those rocks the New England farmers scratched out from the fields centuries ago. Most of all, I had the satisfaction of knowing that we had tapped into a deep American vein of discontent, a mother lode of anger that made people want to change how things are done. Mike Duncannon was a breath of fresh air, a down-to-earth guy who wanted things to be the way they used to be, or at least the way we thought they used to be. He hoped—we all hoped—that New Hampshire was a harbinger of things to come, an early spring for the rebirth of conservatism.

But we still had trouble containing the Loose Duncannon. He went wild in his victory speech. "The peasants are coming with their machetes!" he yelled. As much as he tried to think country, he was still a city boy, and he didn't have the language for the farm. He was trying to invoke pitchforks and Grant

Wood's *American Gothic* but instead conjured images of Mexican rebels, not quite what we were looking for.

The Mod Squad cringed when they heard his speech.

"The line about the peasants—patronizing, *très* patronizing," said Peggy, flipping her highlighted bangs out of her eyes. "I think he's been watching too many movies."

"I think that really bad Pancho Villa movie with Telly Savalas and Chuck Connors was on the other night," I said.

"Machetes! That must be it."

"Maybe they'll call him Blade Frontrunner," quipped Horace, who was as big a movie fan as Barry.

It was worse than we expected. By Wednesday one of the perms had dubbed him "Machete Mike," and at speeches the common folk began showing up swinging machetes. We had to beef up security to keep the blades away from our candidate. In Cheraw, South Carolina, I saw one enterprising young man selling plastic versions from a card table along with buttons that said: "Vote Machete Mike—Slice a CEO Today!"

It was on the Sunday after New Hampshire, on "Face the Nation," that Machete Mike met his alter ego, Stockholder Mike. The perms had dug up all of his investments, which they scrutinized, company by company.

"I'm a family man. Are you gonna blame me for it?" asked Duncannon, trying to put the old Family Value spin on his stock market investments. "I gotta worry about my darling wife's future, so I asked some friends, and they said: 'Get a broker, Mike. Have him invest.' "

And how could he explain that he had substantial stock holdings in many of the corporations he had been lambasting?

Again, Duncannon proved himself to be his own best spin-meister: "Well, at least you know I'm not protecting any-body—even myself!"

Victory is hard to recover from. Nothing about the campaign seemed big enough anymore. The plane we were using before New Hampshire was way too small, so I assigned Gretchen the popsie the task of arranging for a bigger one. We also needed an additional bus for our entourage whenever we touched down. Miraculously, a 727 arrived at the Manchester airport on time to take us and all sixty-some perms off to Columbia, where Duncannon was speaking the next afternoon. Day prac-tically salivated at the idea of having all that up-close time with reporters to keep spinning the victory. I knew she was excited because she even arranged a special brunch the next day for all the staff, one that cost more than the usual Dunkin' Donuts feast.

We landed, and—another miracle—two buses appeared, one for us and one for the perms. I never did get the name of the other hotel they had booked for them. I thought everything was under control, and I was confident enough to order a beer and burger from room service and kick back and watch "Nightline." Ted was interviewing a whole gaggle of liberal analysts who were having fun bashing us as hatemongers. I didn't even care. At about one in the morning I fell into a sound sleep. At exactly 1:45, my phone began ringing and didn't stop for the next two hours.

"Fucking *amateurs!*" It was Pete Dinkins, an AP photogra-pher. "*Fucking amateurs!* Beltway, I am calling you from the lobby of the third shit-ass motel your little moonies have brought us to. They fuckin' can't remember where we're booked!" He hung up, I guess thinking that I could do something about it, but what? I didn't know where that third lobby was, and before I could find my list of pager numbers, the phone was ringing again.

"I'm beginning not to like this campaign," screamed a deep bass voice. "Beltway, it's Tross. Get us the fuck out of here, or send your organizers back to kindergarten. Machete Mike—I like the sound of that!"

"Tross, Tross, so sorry. You know the popsies aren't what they used to be. Back in '92 they could still read. Listen, where are you?"

"Fuckin' Motel 6. Would you really do this to us?"

"What's the deal?"

"They never heard of Mike Duncannon, but they got twelve unoccupied rooms they're willing to give us at the regular rate. Gee, that's only five of us to a room. Ain't America great? Better than the damn Third World countries your candidate keeps screaming about, I guess."

"Tross, relax. Sorry. Let us get the kinks out. Put the nearest popsie on the phone."

"Hello, Harry, it's Grace."

"Grace, what the hell is going on?"

She sounded like she had been crying. "I don't know. No one agreed on what hotel the perms were supposed to go to. No one had written it down, and now we've been driving up and down this highway for hours, stopping at places and asking. Harry, what should we do?"

"Stop driving. Act professional. These guys are gonna write about us from now on. Get them situated, even if it means dropping them off one at a time where they have a room. And apologize profusely. A little free liquor wouldn't hurt."

"Day's gonna kill us," said Grace. "The whole thing is going to cost us twice as much."

"Well, if it had to happen, honey, tonight's the night. Day is pretty much distracted by success. Now, go. Put the perms to bed."

A housing crisis, and Duncannon wasn't even president yet. And now I couldn't fall asleep again. Almost four in the morning. Flipping through the TV channels. *Bob Roberts* was on Bravo. Boy, did they get it wrong in that one. Conservatives are a lot more interesting, and a lot hornier.

And I was. Horny. Might as well admit it. At least I didn't send out for fourteen-year-old choir girls like my granddad.

The phone rang again and I answered, ready to scream at pesky Grace. Instead, I heard Peggy's alto voice. "Harry, I can't sleep, and somehow I had the feeling you couldn't, either. I've got a crick in my neck from the plane. If I come over, will you rub it for me?"

What a line, and what a great idea. Sure, I said, come over. I'm an expert at cricks.

She showed up wearing a red silk kimono—did Mike know how much of his staff wore foreign duds?—and bearing a ceramic carafe with steam coming out of the top.

"Sake," she said. "I always travel with it. You can just pop it in the microwave. It's a very relaxing beverage."

"And so red-blooded American," I said.

"Well, the Japanese aren't all that bad," she said, reaching into her kimono pockets and producing two little cups not much bigger than thimbles. She deftly poured the steaming rice wine and handed me mine. I was sitting on the edge of the bed. Placing her own cup on the floor, she knelt in front of me and began massaging my feet.

"They've got a good work ethic. Ol' Mike is too mean to the Japs," she said, pulling another small vial from her pocket and dabbing my toes with massage oil.

"Umm," I mumbled. I liked it. I had never fully appreciated the true merits of the early Christian preoccupation with feet, but if Peggy wanted to work out her Mary Magdalene complex, that was fine with me. I felt pinned to the edge of the bed as she pressed against my legs with her upper body.

She lowered her head onto my lap, exposing the nape of her neck. "Rub my crick?" she asked. I almost laughed, but she was deadly serious. She continued noodling with my feet. Then, after a few more minutes, she began moving her hands toward my pajama bottom.

"Harry, there's something I've got to tell you before I do this."

"Umm," I said, wondering if there had been more than foot-washing going on in all those biblical scenes. "Sure, what?"

I don't know whether it was the heat of the moment or the heated sake that had carried her into Divine Brown mode, but she never did tell me. I wish she had. Boy, believe me, I wish she had.

A week later I arrived at headquarters to find a truck from Rocco's Capitol Pizza unloading stacks of boxes.

"What is going on here?" I asked.

Horace was royally pissed. "Somebody ordered five hundred pizzas sent here. Some damn joke."

"Who would take an order like that seriously?"

"Rocco would."

"What's the matter with him? Is he crazy?"

"Well, no. Actually, you can't blame him. Seems they got a call from somebody who said he was you. Said we were having a big fund-raiser for the National Fishmongers Association—"

"Fishmongers? Who's ever heard of a fishmonger nowadays?"

"Rocco says he's not surprised to hear of anything in this town anymore. So we're supposed to be having this fishmonger meeting and we need five hundred—get this—five hundred *anchovy* pizzas."

"Oh, God."

"Right. So Rocco didn't necessarily believe it, but then *you* said you'd send along a letter on campaign headquarters stationery and a deposit. Rocco thought that seemed fine. And yesterday he got the letter and he got a check for five hundred dollars. Only it turns out the check is a forgery, and the letterhead was made by cutting the heading off a real letter and color-copying it onto a sheet of blank paper."

"What are we going to do with five hundred pizzas?"

"Do you like anchovies, Harry?"

When I called Duncannon and told him what had happened, he said we'd just have to make good and foot the whole bill. Out of all the people working at campaign headquarters, only four liked anchovy pizza, and we couldn't persuade them to take home more than nine of the things. Horace and I took the other 491 to the nearest homeless shelter, driving in shifts. That evening I noticed the line for dinner at the shelter was a lot shorter than usual.

The next day we got our explanation for the pizza incident. One of the popsies opened a letter addressed to Mike Duncannon. It was rigged with a little friction-ignition gizmo, like striking a match, so that taking the letter out of the envelope lit a short fuse on a small firecracker. She threw it across the room and it went off with a harmless bang, but the noise shook everybody up. The singed note said:

> Hope you enjoyed the snack. Jesus had to make
> do with fishes and loaves, but I thought you and
> your papist friends might prefer a fast-food miracle.
> Free the Fortune 500

"Is something fishy in the Duncannon campaign?" mused one network newscaster in her coverage of the prank. The CEO Bomber might specialize in juvenile antics, but he had a knack for gags that attracted media attention. Even some people within our own organization thought this was a perfect description of Mike Duncannon himself. His whole life proved that he didn't care what others thought about him, so perhaps, on the assumption that even bad publicity is better than no publicity at all. . . . The suspicion made Day all the more determined to hunt down the genuine culprit.

Whoever the CEO Bomber was, and however crazy he

might be, this latest prank touched on a sore point. The religion issue was always a tough one to handle. Popular as JFK had been, it still irked a lot of people that Duncannon was Catholic. They liked it even less in Duncannon. If he leaned one way, he upset half the people; if he leaned too far the other, he turned off the rest. And it was not Duncannon's style to sit quietly in the middle.

We had met lots of Christian Coalition people, made lots of polite chitchat at one function or another. But Russ Reeve and Paul Rogerson—the real powers to be reckoned with—weren't talking. They were staying uncommitted. They could afford to. Separation of church and state and all, they were for the good and the just, values that play no matter who wins. They still might decide to run themselves, but time was getting tight.

Duncannon and I were pulling into a Burger King when Horace phoned to say the coalition wanted to meet. "Reeve's going to be calling you any minute. I just gave his people the number."

"What's it about?" I asked.

"Not a clue."

As soon as I hung up, the phone rang again.

"I'm stepping outside for a minute," Duncannon told me. "Come get me if anyone calls for me." In other words, make 'em wait.

It was Reeve. "This is Russ Reeve. Put Duncannon on."

"Mr. Duncannon has stepped out for a moment. Can I give him a message?"

"Give him the message to step back in and get on the telephone."

He sounded like this was his first and last offer. I waved to Duncannon. "Oh, just a second, Mr. Reeve. Here he comes now."

Duncannon took a deep breath and grabbed the phone. "Hey, Russ. Good of you to call. Yes, I would. When? Is this something urgent? Well, sure, but it's a bit short notice. I can move things around. No problem. Where? What? Hey, Russ, are you planning a hit on me or something? You just like the drama? No, that's fine. Just seems a little strange. Okay, see you."

He handed back the phone. "Couple of crazy bastards. We've got a meeting in forty-five minutes."

"Where?"

"You won't believe this. In the underground parking lot of the Watergate Hotel."

"Why?"

"Don't ask."

The two of them were already waiting in front of their car when we got there. Reeve looked like a businessman. Slightly built, lithe, cold, hard, not a hair out of place. He's one of the few men I've ever met who could wear a black suit without looking like a waiter or an undertaker. He scared me. His expression was cryptic, but penetrating and vaguely menacing. I felt that he knew things about me without being told, and that they weren't nice things, and that he wasn't likely to use them kindly.

Rogerson really looked like a believer. He had a glad-handed honesty that inspired affection and trust. People liked him.

America liked him and showed its affection by making his TV evangelist organization fabulously wealthy and powerful.

We got out of the car and shook hands warily all around.

"You're taking a lot of heat on religious and moral issues," said Reeve.

"Goes with the territory," Duncannon replied.

"We're thinking that Paul should throw his name in again," said Reeve. Testing. He waited.

"He's a good man," Duncannon said. He wouldn't take the bait. "Couldn't ask for anyone better."

"So you think he has a chance, do you?"

Duncannon rubbed his chin. "In the best of all worlds, he ought to have. But here and now, I'm not so sure."

"So you don't think I can win?" Rogerson asked.

"You never know unless you try," said Duncannon.

There was a long silence. A car drove down into the garage, slowed when it saw us, backed up a little, and parked near the entrance. The driver got out—a little too hastily—and hurried back up the ramp, glancing back once or twice. *Great,* I thought. We look like a Mob hit straight out of the movies: two guys in black on one side, a big Irishman on the other, me off to one side, somebody's flunky, dumb with a big gun. Mike Duncannon and the leaders of the Christian Coalition are going to be hauled in by the cops for questioning. Such a good idea to pick a nice secret place to meet.

"Uh, gentlemen," I said, "maybe we'd be less conspicuous if we sat in one of the cars."

We all climbed into the Christian Coalition limousine, which was larger than Duncannon's Cadillac. After a few minutes, I began to notice that somebody smelled bad. Real bad. I guess when you reach a certain position in life nobody tells you things like that anymore, and so you never know. I rolled my window down halfway and poked my nose out, pretending I was giving them token privacy.

Duncannon leaned forward, his hands on his knees. "You really thinking of getting in the race this time around, Paul?" he asked.

"No," said Rogerson. "I don't think it would serve any purpose."

"We've got to proceed cautiously, Mike," Reeve said. "Some people are getting upset about the coalition. The press makes folks think the religious right is the next thing to Waco or Jonestown."

"That's ridiculous."

"Of course it's ridiculous. But those intellectual atheists think anybody who believes in anything is some sort of cult follower."

"So what position do you propose to take?" Duncannon asked.

"If we could support any candidate we liked, Mike, we would support you."

"That's nice to hear. But it sounds like it's not going to happen."

"We're trying to advance our cause, Mike," Reeve said.

"Fair enough."

"In the long term, your cause is not our cause. You're a good man. We admire you. But somewhere down the line there will be a parting of the ways."

"Possibly."

"Probably. In the short term, we need credibility. And you, Mike Duncannon, are a little too extreme. You represent too many of the things that worry people about us."

"Now that's an interesting reason not to support me."

"We're coming out in support of Bill Pineapple. Quite frankly, we think he's going to win the nomination, though we don't think he'll take Jeb Clanton. Given that, we'll get more mileage out of supporting him than supporting you."

"You had to meet me in a garage to tell me you're supporting Bill Pineapple? I could have read that in the paper tomorrow, same as everyone else."

"No, Mike," Rogerson said. "We wanted to let you know that in exchange for coming out in support of Pineapple, we're telling him to play down his attacks on you. We're not coming out for you, but we *are* for you, and if we can help in little ways, behind the scenes, we'll do it. You're our canary in the coal mine. You're testing the waters for us. We're watching to see how you do."

"Great," Duncannon said later in the car as we headed to his house. "I get to sit in a garage all afternoon while two vultures tell me I'm their little bird."

"As long as there's no chance of you actually *getting* the nomination, people like you," Horace told Duncannon in a pow-wow at Duncannon's house later that night.

Duncannon was still shaken by his parking lot experience and wanted to talk about the shifting fortunes of his campaign.

"Tell it to me straight, Horace."

"Okay. People like you because you say what they feel. But they won't *vote* for somebody who says what *they* feel, because they wouldn't vote for *themselves*. They want a president who's more mature and responsible than they are." Horace had to stop talking for a minute to let Duncannon finish laughing. "They say the primaries won't be Duncannon versus Pine-apple, but Duncannon versus non-Duncannon. And most people will be non-Duncannon, because when it comes right down to it they think you might be crazy."

Duncannon had stopped laughing. He looked over at me. "Do you think I'm crazy, Harry?"

"That's what the pundits say the people think, sir. I'm not saying that's what *I* think."

"I know, Harry, but I'm asking what you *do* think."

"I wouldn't be here if I thought you were crazy."

"You might be if you were crazy yourself. Then you wouldn't know any better."

He loved to confuse me, and he was very good at it. I didn't want to get involved in this conversation. I wanted to let Horace manage his ego. "I guess that's a possibility," I conceded.

"Of course, if you were crazy you probably wouldn't know it, and then we would both be crazy together." Duncannon was cheering up again. "Me foolishly looking to you for advice and not getting it because you're crazy, and you admiring a crazy loon like me, also because you're crazy. You know, Harry, I think it's all your fault. Any way you look at it, you must be crazy."

"Thank you for your confidence."

Duncannon laughed and hugged himself and socked me in

the shoulder a couple of times. This bit of blarney was just what it took to clear his head.

"They talk about a glass ceiling for women, Harry, but don't you believe it. Now the powers that be in the old GOP want to convince themselves that there's a ceiling for me, which means they think there's a ceiling for the people, for folks who need jobs, who are struggling against taxes and government and big business, a ceiling for just plain old Americans. . . ."

Suddenly he was off with his speechwriter's knack for turning a familiar old phrase for one thing into a handy tool for himself. What he said didn't make a lot of sense if you paid close attention, but it sang, it rang chords, it inspired. Watching him standing there, smiling, laughing, grabbing huge fistfuls of life as he talked, who could help but want to share some of what he had? Even if he wasn't right, he certainly was alive, which was more than you could say for almost any other candidate.

I can't say we *never* resorted to dirty tricks. But ours were fun, playful, not like the televised name-calling and muckraking of the other candidates.

The papers were filled with Duncannon's remarks about homosexuality. They dredged up columns he wrote ten or twelve years ago about the threat of the gay lifestyle to the health of the nation. Quotes were taken out of context to make him seem insensitive to serious social concerns.

So what if Duncannon didn't like homosexuals? "That's my prerogative," he would say. "If the First Amendment gives every liberal with lips the right to call me a bigot, doesn't the

First Amendment give *me* the right to say that homosexuals are a bunch of unnatural, repugnant, promiscuous, disease-ridden sodomites? I think it does."

One evening when this issue was at its peak, Peggy and I met Barry and Duncannon for drinks on the balcony of the America in Union Station. Duncannon was having a beer and a heaping plate of macaroni and cheese. "Great food," he said. "Just like my mama used to make." Occasionally he slipped one of the pasta tubes over a tine of his fork and flipped it, catapult style, into the rush-hour crowd below.

"Did I ever tell you guys, when I was little we used to throw rocks at cars. When they stopped we pretended they'd just bounced off a wall or something. Played all innocent. Gosh, it was a hoot. We knew how to have fun in those days. We made our own violence, not like today's kids, who just watch it on TV. I love throwing things at people."

His aim was pretty good, too. He particularly liked it when he hit a bald man on the head, then ducked down, pretending to be engrossed in his food when the guy looked up.

"I only aim at Democrats," Duncannon said.

"When in doubt," said an unhappy Barry, "lock and linguini!"

"Sir, this homosexual-bashing image is hurting us," said Peggy.

"I wasn't going to get the faggot vote anyway. I wouldn't worry about it."

"Other people are getting upset about it, too."

"The faggots' friends weren't going to vote for me, either."

"People see you as intolerant."

"Intolerant? What mother-lovin' sonofabitch would call me intolerant?" Duncannon said with a grin. "Just bring him to me and I'll teach him a thing or two. I'm the most tolerant man in the whole wide world, at least among people who think the way I do."

I said I thought we should just ignore the whole issue. It wasn't a big deal, given all the other problems we had.

"No, Harry," Duncannon said, a big grin spreading over his face. "No. Peggy's right. We can't just let it go away. I've got an idea. I think we should *do* something for those homosexuals. If they don't like me, we should encourage them to show it. . . ."

His idea was quite simple. We would encourage—hire, actually—homosexuals to attend opposition campaigns.

"Not Pineapple," Duncannon said. "He's too old. Nobody'd ever make the connection. But how about Kane? You know, there were those stories about his daddy. . . ."

Peggy said she knew some people and would volunteer to set up the show.

Kane was appearing at an outdoor AARP convention in Key West. I went along with Peggy for the ride, and we made ourselves inconspicuous at the back of the crowd. It was Kane's kind of audience: old and prosperous, looking for stability and a little bit of quiet. They were beyond caring about abortion. Foreign trade to them meant Mercedes and Jaguars. They didn't even care much about immigration, just as long as the waiters at the country club were polite. Kane seemed a little young and inexperienced to be president, but he looked like a good boy and came from a nice family.

"Tell your children and grandkids to vote for me," Kane said. He wore lemon-colored trousers, white shoes and belt, and a madras shirt, and toyed with a golf club as though he really played.

The biggest cheers came when he reminded the old folks that he wasn't there to ask them for money, because he had saved up and financed his campaign out of his own allowance—something many of them clearly wished their own children had the sense to do.

Kane was really starting to relax. He even used the golf club to launch into an Ed McMahon impersonation, wringing a nostalgic tear out of his audience as they all wondered what the country had become without Johnny.

Then they arrived. The gay brigade.

I didn't know what Peggy's connections were, but she had found the most flamingly gay queens Florida could muster, and paid them fifty bucks apiece to have a little fun.

First came half a dozen well-proportioned men in ultra-skimpy bathing suits. They would have been hunks in any girl's book but for the heavy makeup, limp wrists, and Jessica Rabbit swish to their walk. They carried placards that read: QUEENS FOR KANE FOR PRESIDENT. A dozen gays in cheerleader outfits, large gold K's emblazoned on their chests, did the can-can—or "Kane-Kane," as they called it—to a hopped-up tune of "Hail to the Chief." Next came a small mob dressed in outrageous outfits—there were only forty-two of them, according to Peggy's expense sheet, though it seemed like ten times that many. They started working the crowd of stupefied retirees.

"Isn't Orson Kane just the dreamiest man you've ever seen?"

"Do you know, that bad Mr. Duncannon doesn't want people like us around. I hope you'll make sure *he* never gets into office."

"Hey, mister, you're kind of cute. Want to ditch the wife and try a little January–December romance with me?"

"I like Pineapple, too. He's a *succulent* fruit!"

Well, the crowd evaporated pretty quickly. Kane did his best to keep calm and maintain order, but he didn't know what was going on and there was no good way out of it. He was damned if he told the gays to stay and damned if he tried to get rid of them.

The press did not give the incident much coverage, and the gay community in Florida apologized to Kane for the inexplicable display. It really didn't accomplish much, but Duncannon was happy. He was, after all, just having a little fun, like throwing macaroni and rocks.

Bill Pineapple, I'd heard, had a great sense of humor. I don't know why he always seemed so dull in public. Horace, who had spent a lot of time at official functions, told me that Pineapple once saw Jimmy Carter, Gerald Ford, and Richard Nixon entering a room together. "Uh-oh," said Pineapple. "Here comes See No Evil, Hear No Evil, and Evil."

Evil showed up one night in Florida, where we were campaigning in Key Largo. Duncannon had visited a junior high school, then gone to an Elks meeting later that night. When we got to the Sheraton, they had lost our reservation, and there weren't enough rooms for all nine of us. "No problem," said Duncannon, who was feeling very good because the Elks had given him a standing ovation. "We can double up. Harry, you're my roomie for the night!"

I hate sharing a room with someone I'm not sleeping with, so I dreaded what the night would bring. But the place was spacious, with two queen-size beds. At first, it was fun. It was getting late and the Elks' rubber chicken hadn't made much of an impact on our stomachs, so we called room service for nachos and beers. Duncannon channel-surfed, looking for his own sound bites, and was happy to catch a shot of himself engulfed by happy grade-school students.

Then things got weird. From out of his garment bag Duncannon produced an Ouija board and laid it on the bed. "Harry, it's time to say good night to Dick."

I didn't want to make a scene. I really hoped this wasn't going to be some strange sex thing. But then Duncannon also set up, right next to the Ouija board, a picture of Richard Nixon in his familiar, nerdy victory pose—arms extended above his head, accentuating his narrow shoulders.

"Dick, are you there? We're right near where you and Bebe used to hang out. Give us a high sign, Mr. President."

The bed began to shake. I looked over to see if there was a Magic Fingers involved, but the headboard sported no such equipment. The chocolate mints fell off the pillows. "Get over here, Harry. He's tryin' to say something!"

I plunked myself down next to him on his bed and put my fingers lightly on the other side of the little gliding thing, which began migrating around the board. F-L-O-R-I-D-A L-O-S-E, it spelled out letter by letter at a tedious pace.

"Whaddya mean, lose? Should I give up?" shouted Duncannon, pushing at the board. N-O, the glider spelled out.

"No!" screamed a voice from the television, which had been left on as background noise. Duncannon and I turned to the set, where CNN anchors had been replaced by a black-and-white ghost. It was Richard Nixon.

"They'll have Mike Duncannon to kick around for a long time," said the staticky voice as the image flickered on the screen. Only the broad, turned-up nose was truly recognizable.

"But what should I do?" asked Duncannon, who seemed ridiculously comfortable with the idea of talking to a dead ex-boss on a television set at the Sheraton.

"Wait," said the flickering ghost. "Wait."

"Wait," Duncannon repeated. Then without explanation, he got up, went into the bathroom, brushed his teeth, returned, and climbed in between the covers of his bed. Within minutes he was sound asleep, leaving me to flip frantically through the channels, trying to convince myself that it had been a joke.

The next day he never mentioned anything about it. *Maybe he had been put up to it,* I thought, *by Gary or the Mod Squad. Maybe the Elks had slipped him a few drinks I hadn't seen. Maybe there had been electromagnetic storms in the area. Or maybe he—or I—was crazy.*

6

Dateline: Georgia, a few days after the Ouija "summit." I had looked forward to my first day off in many weeks. Not a single event had been scheduled that day. It was downtime before the big push toward Atlanta resumed on Monday. I could spend hours and hours doing absolutely nothing. In the middle of the afternoon I actually decided to take a nap in my motel room. I hung the "Do Not Disturb" sign outside, took the phone off the hook, and settled down, feeling more decadent than I had in years.

About fifteen minutes later, the door to my room flew open.

My first thought was that it was a dream.

My second thought was that I was about to be seduced, perhaps raped, by a member of the Duncannon family.

My third was that I should get the hell out of there.

My fourth thought was that I couldn't: I was stark naked under the stiff motel sheets, and naked was not how I cared to face Day Duncannon.

After that, things happened so fast that I lost count.

"Hiya, Harry," she said, too sweetly. "Are we having a little rest?"

Something was seriously wrong. Did she know about Sherry and me? Was she about to kill me? In her outback vest and hat she looked a little like Crocodile Dundee.

"How did you get in here?" I asked.

"Need you ask, Harry? This is Day, remember. I have my ways. I've never known you to lounge around in the daytime. Thought maybe you were drunk or seriously hung over, so I brought you a cup of coffee," she said, removing the plastic lid.

"Thanks," I said, miserable. I reached for the Styrofoam cup. She let go an instant too soon. For a hundredth of a second it fell through the air, steaming hot, right over my crotch. My fingers grabbed it just in time.

"Say, Harry, you can move pretty fast when you've got something important to save," she said in fake wonder. "Well, Harry, we're in *deep doody*. If we're going to save the Mike Duncannon campaign, you had better get your sorry ass out of that bed and into the car in about twelve seconds. We have got to scoop some major poop."

No one can get washed, shaved, and dressed in twelve seconds, but with Day Duncannon urging me along, I made it in just over thirteen.

"What's up?" I asked, climbing into the car.

At last I understood why the Duncannon family was famous for wrecking cars, why local auto dealers adored them and competed for their business. One Cadillac-Oldsmobile dealership sent Pop Duncannon a joke promotion flier: "Buy fifty cars and get the next one free!!!" I still had one foot on the pavement when Day floored the accelerator. We must have been up to forty by the time she shot over the curb, grazed a fire hydrant, skidded across two lanes of dense traffic, and headed toward the local campaign headquarters.

"They've got tapes," she said between gritted teeth.

"I thought that videotape mess was over and done," I said.

"Not videotapes. Audiotapes."

"Audiotapes?" I was baffled.

"AUDIOtapes!"

"What kind of audiotapes?" I asked.

"Audiotapes with sound," she said sarcastically. Wheels screaming, horn blaring, she swerved around some yuppie bimbo in a Saab turbo. "You ever notice that the worst drivers in the world drive Saab turbos, Harry? I'd like to go back and pound that bitch, but there's never enough time in life to do all the little things that mean so much."

"Day, tell me about these tapes."

"Some chambermaid at the Willard has a tape recorder, and she likes to walk up and down the hall with it on. Now she would like to *share* what she heard with the world."

"Shit. Any clue what it is?"

"That dumb bastard! Well, if it's going to make the news, it can't be good. She's going on the air in five minutes. CNN. Followed by the feast. Those bloodsucking reporters got their appetizer last time, but they were gypped out of the main course, so you can bet they're real hungry for a bite of Mike Duncannon's butt now."

Our Atlanta office was packed. Day plowed through the press and the popsies like a battleship through a wading pool. I followed in her wake, smiling and nodding benevolently as reporters shoved microphones in my face. Nobody shoved microphones at Day Duncannon. Not since that little incident last week. Crowds made her nervous, she said. Her arms just went sort of twitchy. She sure hoped that gal from Channel 8 got the wires out of her jaw and could get back to work real soon.

Duncannon and the Mod Squad were holed up in the war room. The big-screen TV was tuned to an ESPN-2 rebroadcast of Georgetown vs UConn. Sherry hung on her husband's left arm, sobbing quietly and dabbing at her mascara with a handkerchief. Duncannon held the remote control high in the air while Horace struggled to grab it.

"Sir, that press conference is going to start any minute," Horace protested.

"Just hold your horses, Horace," Duncannon chuckled. "Just one more second while we mush those UConn Huskies way up north where they belong."

"Give him the remote, Mike," Day boomed.

Duncannon turned. "Awwww, Day . . ."

Day had an ace up her sleeve. "Brandy Gecko and I watched the game last night. Georgetown lost by a point. Now give him the remote."

Duncannon surrendered the remote with a forlorn sigh. "Horace, that big, tall brother of yours is really screwing up our team. Losing to UConn, of all places. Hell's bells."

The press conference was just beginning. A pretty red-haired woman in her thirties stood looking nervously at the camera. The caption: "Molly O'Shaughnessy, Chambermaid, Willard Hotel" swam below her on the screen.

"What did you do to that woman, Mike?" Day demanded.

"I didn't do a thing to her. Talked to her a few times in the hall, that's all. Whatever she says, it's a lie."

The Chambermaid's Tale began. "I used to see Mr. Duncannon regularly at the hotel. He was always coming in just around the time I was making up the rooms, and he'd sometimes stop in the hall to chat. He was a very nice gentleman."

"Well, I take it back," Duncannon said. "The woman speaks the truth."

An off-screen interviewer asked, "What did Mr. Duncannon talk about, Ms. O'Shaughnessy?"

"Oh, he just said things like how nice it was to see real Americans working at menial jobs instead of a bunch of foreigners who can't even speak the language. And he asked if I had children. I told him I have two boys."

"Did he talk to you about your boys?"

"He asked where they went to school. I said I sent them to a religious school, because I wanted the best for my sons. So then he said that when he's president he'll put God back in the public schools so that all Americans can grow up Christian the way they should."

"And what did you think of that, Ms. O'Shaughnessy?"

"I didn't like it very much."

"And why is that, Ms. O'Shaughnessy?"

"I'm Jewish. My boys go to yeshiva."

"Jewish? With a name like Molly O'Shaughnessy?"

"O'Shaughnessy is the name the immigration people gave my father when his family came over from Russia. Our real name was something like Oshinsky—I'm not really sure. I was named Molly after my bubbe Malka."

Duncannon looked like he was going to faint. "Saints preserve us. A Jewish Molly O'Shaughnessy!"

The interviewer continued. "I understand that you have some tape recordings, Ms. O'Shaughnessy?"

The woman looked down toward the floor and shifted from foot to foot. "Well, I was worried. I—I don't know . . ." She looked as though she were going to cry. "I had a little tape recorder. I know it was wrong. I don't know why I did it. . . ."

"I can tell you why she did it," Barry said. "She does it all the time. I had people look into her. She peddled tapes on Senator Klopstock last year. Mixed up in some Chinese fiasco, too—secret trade agreement information that got leaked to a multinational. She even tried to implicate Gordy Hedge in a sex scandal, only nobody would believe it."

Day pounded her fist on the desk. "That's all well and good. We can smear her from here to eternity, but that doesn't help *us* much if the tapes are any good."

"Now let's listen to excerpts from Ms. O'Shaughnessy's tapes of Mike Duncannon at the Willard Hotel," said the interviewer. A still photograph of Duncannon appeared on the screen. They had picked a shot with a grin on his face. Under other circumstances he would look endearing. In this context he looked like a man capable of anything, leering in wicked delight. A transcript of the scarcely audible words flashed over his face.

MAN: My dear, one day soon I will rule this land, and you will be my lovely queen.

WOMAN: Oh, darling. But what will [inaudible]. . . .

MAN: [laughs] Him? Ha! I've taken care of him already. The fool! They'll never find the body.

WOMAN: You are so wonderful, my love. You can do anything. I've looked forward to this for so long—to the day when we can be together openly, when we no longer have anything to hide.

MAN: We won't fear anyone. Those little people will regret the way they've treated me. They will regret it. . . .

Mike Duncannon stood with his mouth wide open. Horace and Barry gasped.

Sherry looked uncomprehendingly at her husband. Her hand dropped from his arm. "Who is that woman? How could you do this to me?" As the tears welled up in her eyes, she hauled off and landed a right uppercut square on his jaw. She was a true Duncannon after all—and she hadn't even been born one.

He knew how to take a punch. He didn't flinch, just wiped at the trickle of blood with the back of his sleeve.

"Sherry, my little Petunia," he started, but she was already out the door.

Day looked like she wanted to kill him. "You fool! You FOOL! How could you let somebody overhear you? Don't you ever learn anything?"

Duncannon was slowly beginning to shake off the glassy-eyed look. Jewish O'Shaughnessys, taped conversations, a sock in the jaw from his beautiful wife—it was a lot for any man to take.

Day was angry enough to burst but had enough sense to

keep her voice down. "I don't give a rat's ass if you want to shack up with some floozy, murder Toad Gecko, and turn America back into a monarchy. That is *fine* with me. Just hunky-dory. But how could you babble your fool head off like that in a downtown Washington hotel room, at the top of your lungs, right next to the door?!"

"But . . . but . . ." Mike Duncannon's gift of gab had momentarily abandoned him.

"All my work for nothing," Day went on. "I knew I should have run for president myself. Just taken all that 'Duncannon for President' stuff and used it where it would do some good."

Horace and Alan seemed to be wondering whether to clean out their desks tomorrow or right away.

Something bothered me. In the back of my mind was a faint murmur. My memory was trying to tell me something, but what?

It was my darling Peggy who asked the crucial question: How did we know the voice was Mike Duncannon's? "It was pretty faint. The quality wasn't very good. It could have been anybody," she said.

It could have been anybody. She was right. I turned to Sam Magillicuddy.

"Sam, did you get that on tape?" I said.

"Sure thing, Harry."

"Play it again, Sam."

He started rewinding the VCR. "You a glutton for punishment or something, Harry?"

"No," I said. "There's something wrong here."

Sam played it again.

"Play it again, Sam," I said.

He did.

"Again."

Everyone was looking at me. Even Day had fallen silent.

Play it again, I thought. Play it again, Sam. Movies. That was it. "That's not Mike Duncannon!" I said.

"I could have told you that," said Duncannon.

"Well, then, why the hell didn't you?" Day asked.

It was a movie soundtrack on the tape. Whether she knew it or not, Molly O'Shaughnessy had tape-recorded a movie.

"Does that conversation sound familiar to you, sir?" I asked Duncannon.

"No, Harry, I just told you it wasn't me."

"No, that's not what I mean. Do you remember hearing those lines in a movie you watched in your room?"

Duncannon scratched his head. "Well, no, but I usually doze off during movies. Sherry likes those, sort of—well, you know—those girl movies, and they just don't keep me awake."

Day was back in action. "Who can we get as an expert on this? Leonard Maltin?"

"Maybe we should keep it a little more quiet," Peggy suggested.

"I had a friend in high school," Duncannon said. "We called him Soldier Boy because he never could stand up straight. All he did was drink beer, beat people up, and watch movies. He runs a video store out in Chevy Chase. He'll help us, if he knows what's good for him."

About a week later, months after he disappeared, Toad Gecko was back in Washington. The Duncannon brothers thought it was a good time to make him reappear. But Gecko was a kinder, gentler Toad, a quieter Toad. He had become reserved, polite. There was no denying that Toad Gecko was also a much handsomer man. He had lost about forty pounds and gained a neck and waist. A new strong, resolute jawline made him seem younger and more forceful, despite the fact that he tended to jump at loud noises and flinch when strangers approached.

His first ad was for The Gap, but others followed quickly until you couldn't open any magazine without seeing Toad Gecko's face with a milk moustache or hawking cologne or something, and those HMO billboards were becoming distressingly inescapable. He did guest shots on "Murphy Brown" and "The Simpsons," and finally landed a recurring role on "Tomorrow Is Another Day of Our Lives," the new soap opera based on *Gone With the Wind*. (We were surprised when Brandy invited Day to one of her brother's cast parties, but it seemed that the two women had been spending a lot of time together.)

"You won't have Toad to kick around anymore," Gecko said at the press conference in which he announced he was resigning from the House. Everybody missed him. He had brought a little color to American politics. But now Mike Duncannon was here and he wasn't needed. A little later, in a gesture most people thought was a final capitulation to the mainstream GOP, but which we recognized as a last personal act of defiance, he came out in support of Bill Pineapple.

Soldier Boys Town Video was in the worst section of Chevy Chase, squeezed between a gym and a bar, the perfect location for its proprietor. He cringed when we walked in.

"Oh, shit. I didn't do it, Day, I really didn't do it, I swear on my mother's grave," he said, backing away until he collided with the Kung Fu movie rack. His store specialized in sex and blood movies. A small rack of classics included *Deep Throat* and *Behind the Green Door*. The Foreign Film section displayed *Emmanuelle* and *Snuffing Sluts in South America*.

"Yeah, nice to see you, too, Soldier Boy," Day said.

In spite of his revolting appearance, Soldier Boy was a whiz when it came to movies.

"*King for a Day*," he said after hearing the tape a single time. "1967, I think. A real stinkeroo, starring a bunch of nobodies." He consulted a catalog. "It is available on video. If you'd like I can order it for you for $29.95. Add a ten-buck rush charge and I'll get it in twenty-four hours."

"Thanks, Soldier Boy," Day said. "We owe you."

"Yeah, anytime," he said. "Hey, Day, tell Mike I said hi. We should go out and get shit-faced one of these days, just like old times. And if he needs a new FCC commissioner or something after he gets elected, tell him to give me a call."

We drove to Charleston in a light rain for Duncannon's visit to the Tower. We were counting on the visit to get us back on track. We had been putting out fires for weeks, and now it was time to work on our positive image. The school administration was leery. They worried that he might say something outrageous and draw humiliating national attention to the place. But they didn't want to antagonize Duncannon either—he was potentially a very good friend.

The cadets loved him. And why not? He was pro-military,

pro-South, pro-keeping the women out of the Tower and in the kitchen where they belong, cooking and cleaning for their big strong men and tending to their broods of Christian babies.

A few hundred cadets skipped classes to stand in the rain and listen to Duncannon's talk.

"Lock and load!" he yelled to the perfect audience. They cheered as though he had said the cleverest thing in the world. "Lock and load!" he yelled again.

"You boys know that a lot of folks—mostly folks up North, of course—think you ought to let women into the Tower. They figure now that they let boys wear dresses and swish around and get married to each other, why, it's only fair to let the women be soldiers. They figure that they have women soldiers over in Israel and they have women soldiers in China, so what's good enough in *those* countries should be good enough for the U.S. of A."

There were murmurs of unhappiness in the audience.

"Well *I* don't *think* so." Cheers. "No, gentlemen, I *do not* think so. Can you picture girls landing at Omaha Beach? Girls at Iwo Jima? Sounds like a pictorial feature in some pornographic magazine. Girls in the Civil War. You know, it wouldn't have been 'brothers fighting against brothers,' but 'brothers against sisters,' 'mothers fighting daughters.' Kinda changes your image of war."

"Yeah! Yeah!" yelled the cadets. They adored him.

"Where do you find a tampon dispenser out in the jungle?" He lowered his voice to a stage whisper. "How do you squat down to pee in terrain infested with scorpions and snakes? We guys are safe up *here*, but women . . ." He shook his head.

"You know that fungus you get on your feet? Well, women get it—ah, you don't want to know. And do you really want somebody with PMS commanding a battalion, maybe invading some poor innocent country just because her hormones are off that day?"

No wonder the Tower had been concerned about Duncannon's appearance. The cadets were having a great time, but the perms who trailed us were having an even better one. You could tell by the smiles on their faces that they could almost taste the stories they would file.

"And you know that time-honored part of the physical exam? That moment you all so fondly remember, when they grab your family jewels and tell you to cough? Now how the hell is a woman going to do that?"

This was Mike Duncannon at his best and worst. He knew exactly how to work a crowd. The consummate entertainer. But he was made for vaudeville, not for the evening news. A hundred years earlier a tireless stumper like him would have killed everywhere and taken the nation. Modern technology had its drawbacks, though. What worked at the Tower would never play in Carmel.

"You know, guys, this political campaigning is a lot like war. A lot like the Civil War." A pause. A drop in the register of his voice to something more serious, almost reverent. "A lot like the Civil War *could* have been. I won't be stopped, lads. Lock and load!" They knew the routine and let out a cheer. "Lock and load!" they yelled as one.

"We're striking North!" Duncannon said. "Maryland lays wide open and will be ours! We'll take New York, Connecticut,

Massachusetts. We've already got New Hampshire, now we'll sweep clear through the rest of the Northeast. And then we'll settle the rest of the country. We'll open up the farmlands of the Midwest, and push toward the coast, through Utah, Nevada, and California. We will be pioneers all over again, forging a nation where the brave and the strong and the good survive. But this time—" he paused, his face gleaming with the triumph of the righteous, and he seemed to grow in stature before our eyes. "This time, we will do it *right*!"

Word of Duncannon's innocence in the tape incident got out to the press quickly, but a simple denial wasn't going to erase that image of a pretty Irish-Jewish lassie and her tape recorder lurking in the halls. We needed a big counterevent to replace it on people's TV screens and in their minds. Barry wanted "Nightline," but Horace and Peggy won out for going straight to Leno.

"Let's not dignify this by making it news," Horace said. "Let's show it for what it really is: farce."

Leno's people went for it. The network hyped the event in prime-time spots for two days: "Is Mike Duncannon plotting to take over the world? Tune in tomorrow night."

Horace and Peggy spent a day with Soldier Boy assembling a medley of old movie clips, which Peggy presented on the "Tonight" show. She was attractive, professional—and perfectly deadpan. Jay Leno warmed to her immediately.

"Jay, Ms. Molly O'Shaughnessy presented tapes she made that revealed Mike Duncannon's secret machinations. Here, let me remind people of the scandal that shook our nation." She played the excerpt from *King for a Day*, the sound starting against a black screen, then the picture fading in. The audience and Leno laughed.

"Jay," Peggy continued with a straight face, "I'm sorry to say that Ms. O'Shaughnessy did not reveal the total extent of Mike Duncannon's secret life. There were other tapes that she suppressed. I feel it is my civic duty to show them now."

Leno appeared suitably shocked and concerned.

"In this recording, Mike Duncannon was having a secret meeting with representatives of the former Soviet Union . . ."

Ninotchka, with Melvyn Douglas and Greta Garbo.

". . . and in secret negotiations with France."

The "Marseillaise" rises as Humphrey Bogart and Claude Rains walk across the runway in the closing scene of *Casablanca*.

"And Ms. O'Shaughnessy captured this while plumping the pillows as Mike Duncannon took a shower in his hotel room . . ."

Gene Kelly's *Singin' in the Rain* number.

"He has a lovely singing voice, you know. Almost reminds you of someone."

There was a silence as the next clip started up. Peggy looked baffled until the picture faded in. "Oh, right—that's D. W. Griffith's *America*. It's a silent film."

She paused. "But, you know, he always tries to stick up for the little people."

Errol Flynn as Robin Hood.

"And his constituents know that, whatever his flaws, he is a good-hearted person who deserves their support."

Closing scene from *It's a Wonderful Life*.

"But, of course, Mike Duncannon is not just Mike Duncannon."

Superman ripping open his Clark Kent clothing.

"And as for all that other nonsense, those ridiculous accusations that Mike Duncannon was plotting and philandering and whatever else, I recorded a personal message from Mr. Duncannon himself to Molly O'Shaughnessy:"

The final scene of *Gone With the Wind*: "Frankly . . . [a quick cut to Mike Duncannon saying "Molly"] . . . I don't give a damn."

Peggy had performed brilliantly. I couldn't stop telling her how beautiful she looked onscreen. Polls the next day showed a complete turnaround in public opinion on the duplicity of Mike Duncannon. In fact, the Soldier Boy cut-and-paste show was so successful that for a while afterward it became a recurring technique on comedy shows and in the humor segments of local news programs.

Duncannon had a replica Oscar made up for Soldier Boy inscribed, BEST RESCUE.

The clock read 3:30 A.M. in my room at the Holiday Inn in Baton Rouge. I blearily picked up my ringing phone. I knew it would be Peggy—she'd taken to calling me late at night and treating me to her version of phone sex, which was to read from the diaries of Anaïs Nin.

It was Peggy, but she wasn't feeling amorous. "Holy shit," she breathed into the phone. "*He* was here."

"Who's he?"

"Duncannon. Well, maybe I should say *they* were here. He

just buzzed me from the lobby. Said he had his friend Dick Nixon with him and they wanted to stop up for a nightcap."

"What did you say?"

"I told him I didn't have anything, and I wasn't decent. He said maybe they'd stop by another time. Harry, has he started hitting the booze hard or something?"

"No. He's just tired. He's running on empty. He needs a rest. And so do you. Don't worry about it. Go to sleep."

I stayed up the rest of the night.

I knew there was something wrong when I got back from Louisiana because Barry Orenstein asked me out to lunch. Barry never seemed to have much time for anybody. I liked him—everybody did—but he was the odd duck of the office, the Jew in the enemy camp, like Joseph working for Pharaoh. He kept to himself, always analyzing his figures, preparing memos about image and demographic groups for Day. He had a wife and three kids in Silver Spring, so he almost never went out for drinks at the end of the day.

We went to Krupin's and ordered pastrami sandwiches and Cel-Ray sodas. "My soul food," said Barry. "Listen, Harry, I asked you here because I'm worried about the whole campaign. I don't think Mike is all there."

"What do you mean? If you're talking about that thing where he compared 'We Shall Overcome' to a Broadway show tune, well, that's just vintage Mike. Nothing we can do about it but pray."

"No, that's not it. I've gotten used to vintage Mike. It's Mike's new imaginary friend I can't stand."

"Imaginary friend?"

"Dick. Little Dick Nixon." Yikes. I had been doing advance work in Ohio when Mike and Barry were traveling together in Tennessee. Mike must have packed his Ouija board. What was I supposed to say?

I tried acting casual, amused. "So he gave you the Dead Tricky Dick trick?"

Barry was stone-faced. "He really believes that shit, you know. He believes that he gets special messages, just for him, from a recently dead president."

"Oh, come on," I said. "He does not. He's just having a little fun, that's all. He's pulled that joke on me, too. He had you going, didn't he?"

Barry had made a decision, although I wouldn't know until later just how drastic it was.

"I can take him being a charlatan and a bigot and an extremist," he said. "But a psychic nut? I don't think so."

The CEO Bomber struck for the third time the day after Super Tuesday.

We lost in all seven states. Naturally we felt down, but we were far from being out. Given the odds against us, the way the party was closing ranks, we were doing okay. Duncannon simply laughed when anyone suggested that he ought to pull out.

"Pull out? Now why on earth would I want to do that?" he asked. "I don't know about you, but a setback to me just means we need to work a little harder. We are going to stop Bill Pineapple. Let him try to shut us out. We'll kick down the door and crash that old Republican party. I haven't met the bouncer yet who can keep out a Duncannon who wants to get in."

If Duncannon didn't capture the Republican nomination, he sure wouldn't rule out a third-party ticket. And then there was always 2000. Whatever happened, we were a *long* way from the end. "Duncannon's Dragoons" fight best against heavy odds, he said, plowing through the crowd like a conquering hero, hugging the popsies, socking shoulders, beaming with pleasure. No one would have guessed that this was a man they said had just lost big.

"Yup! We've got 'em worried, guys," he said to the assembled troops. "They're on the run." He laughed. "So what if they're running way, way, *way* ahead of us? You ever heard of the Tortoise and the Hare? Well, we'll catch him. And I'm planning a little dinner party after California—hare with pineapple garnish, an old Duncannon family favorite. We'll serve it on a tablecloth stitched together from those Howdy Doody shirts I bought so cheap. Yes, this game is *far* from over."

Day, meanwhile, was on the phone trying to get control over compromising statements from enemies *and* friends. One of the networks erroneously reported that Pop Duncannon had been an ardent Father Coughlin fan, while good old Darryl Dent was loudly claiming credit for handing his dear friend Mike Duncannon a big piece of Louisiana on a plate.

Suddenly, all hell broke loose.

One of the popsies screamed. We looked up to see a dark green, late-model Cadillac bearing down on campaign headquarters at full tilt—though police investigators later said it was doing no more than twenty. The driver stared straight ahead, expressionless, as though in a daze. People flung themselves out of the way as the car smashed through the front door and plowed through fifteen feet of desks. As the car ground to a halt against the back wall, the driver slumped against his now limp airbag.

Barry and I started forward to help the occupant when dense bluish smoke and an overpowering stench began billowing out of the car's windows and trunk. Barry ducked low and bravely continued on his rescue mission, coughing and fanning the smoke from his face. Then he stopped suddenly, turned, and headed for the sidewalk, gulping in huge breaths of fresh air.

"It's a dummy!" he shouted. "Everybody get out!"

The rotten egg smell that poured from the car was so overwhelming that we all retreated half a block away. There was no flame, but smoke continued to come out of the crumpled car until firefighters in gas masks crept close and pumped the vehicle full of chemical foam, which seeped out to the sidewalk in unworldly blue malodorous puddles.

The driver of the car was nothing but the torso and arms of a store mannequin with a picture of Mike Duncannon's face taped to the head. A video camera and transmitter affixed to the dashboard enabled whoever was responsible to steer the car with a sophisticated remote mechanism. There was enough gadgetry and know-how involved that the cops thought they would surely find some good lead to the CEO Bomber. The interior of the car was packed with blue-colored signal flares and stink bombs wired into a simple ignition system. There were also a couple of mirrors, whose presence was explained by the note staple-gunned to the driver-dummy's chest:

> Blue smoke and mirrors and a great big stink.
> That's you, Mike Duncannon.
>
> Free the Fortune 500

Fortunately, outside of a few bumps and scratches sustained while vaulting over desks, no one was injured. Campaign headquarters, however, was a disaster. Tens of thousands of dollars' worth of equipment had been smashed or ruined by the smoke and chemical extinguisher. Everything else was so permeated by the foul odor that no one could bear to use it. Even after we moved to new quarters, the few essential items we salvaged—no matter how much they were aired—carried enough of the smell that it followed us forever. New visitors to headquarters always crinkled their noses in mild disgust.

This dangerous juvenile prank had a powerful and lasting effect. The press loudly denounced such acts of terrorism or vandalism. Nonetheless, reporters delighted in the opportunity the incident provided; for several weeks afterward, every article or news report on the Duncannon campaign was guaranteed to have some stupid wordplay on fragrant, odor, smell, stink, aroma, or the like. "Duncannon Stinks" buttons, scratch-and-sniff Duncannon postcards, and car air fresheners in the shape of Duncannon's head sprung up at all the political novelty stands.

Duncannon responded in typical fashion. "Whoever you are, you're a coward," he said at a press conference. "It was only your dumb luck that nobody got hurt, and next time we might not all be so lucky. If you don't like me, if you've got something against me, then you come have it out with me. Leave my staff alone. Leave innocent people alone. I've never backed down from a fight in my life, and I'll meet you anytime, anywhere, and we can duke it out one on one."

The press and the police criticized Duncannon for such provocative remarks, but a lot of people responded. He was Gary Cooper. He was Spencer Tracy. He was the American spirit.

The FBI investigation of the CEO Bomber lagged. The agency offices were clogged with crackpots begging to confess—some for the glory, others hoping to claim the CEO Bomber Defense Fund, which, with the stock market soaring, was now worth $92 million.

On March 20, a week after the latest attack, fifty-four-year-old John Jacob Simon was arrested on the steps of the Capitol. He was dressed in a giant parrot suit, haranguing passersby with vehement anti-Duncannon tirades and passing out leaflets that ended with "Free the Fortune 500."

Simon was the former CEO of the Axtrixx Corporation, a company that traded international licensing rights to American technology in exchange for shoddy foreign consumer products. He had resigned this position to join the 1992 Russ Parrot presidential campaign, an experience that evidently unhinged him. According to former business associates, Simon took to proclaiming that "business is the one true religion." He called the New York Stock Exchange the "American Vatican," and held Spreadsheet Study Groups in a plush, mahogany-paneled shrine in his basement, where a small coterie of deranged businessmen prayed to an ivory statue of Russ Parrot, the "Corporate Messiah." His most recent obsession was that Mike Duncannon represented the evil Anti-Parrot, sent to plunge the world into a dark age of populism.

The CEO Bomber Defense Fund reassembled the old O.J. Dream Team to represent Simon. There was talk that, after his acquittal, he may be invited to found a CEO's Union, an organization to protect big business against oppression by the labor force and persecution at the hands of politicians who don't know which side America's bread is buttered on.

Russ Parrot himself had been surprisingly quiet throughout the present campaign, wondering whether to throw his ten-gallon hat back in the ring, but not committing himself one way or the other. Political advisers suggested that he take up a more productive pastime, such as collecting Hummel figures or twiddling his thumbs. But Simon's fervent display was just what it took to push Parrot over the brink.

"Where there is one looney," he cried, "there is a whole bin full of loonies. I have found my constituency again!" He declared his candidacy.

"Well, I am awfully glad to hear that," Duncannon said when he heard the news. "This campaign needs a little comic relief, and with Locke, Atwater, and Kane gone, we were running low on funny men. Pineapple is not the least bit funny, and I can't be expected to do *everything*."

Publicly, Duncannon lamented the whole sorry affair. At a mass ILGWU rally in Newark, New Jersey, he alluded to the CEO Bomber pranks. "We are thankful that this is over. Our sympathy and our prayers go out to Mr. Simon and his family and friends. In spite of his actions, we must remember that he, too, was a victim. The vicious world of big business ruined him, drove him to the brink of psittacosis—ooops, no, I'm sorry, that's parrot fever—to the brink of psychosis, I meant to say." He shook his head sadly, but those in front could see him chuckle.

"But, of course, our sympathy and prayers go out even more to the working people of America, whose lives are increasingly ruled by crazy CEOs like Mr. Simon. Simon says, 'You're fired,' and forty thousand workers head home to their hungry families. Simon says, 'Let's cut costs and increase profits,' and more American jobs are handed over to sweatshop coolies in Taiwan. Simon says, 'Get Mike Duncannon,' and all his little CEO pals say yes, they will. Well, I don't do what Simon says. I don't play that game. *America* won't play that game anymore. We've got work to do! We're going to take this country back for honest, God-fearing people!"

7

The night was memorable for so many things, it's hard to know where to start. I had never attended an official pro-life rally, even though I had spent so much of my youth at religious gatherings. When I was growing up, Christians were naturally against abortion. They just weren't so . . . LOUD . . . about it. My grandfather and his fellow preachers never would have held up placards with pictures of fetuses. It would have been considered tasteless, rude, even anti-Christian. Abortion was a filthy, disgusting thing. Abortion was a sin. End of discussion.

So imagine my befuddlement when I entered the circus-like atmosphere of the COWS FLOP—Christian Organized Women Standing For Life, Opportunity, and Purity held in an indoor rodeo arena in Oklahoma. Outside the arena there was a carnival set up with games and prizes. There was, of course, cow-flop bingo, with several unfortunate bovines standing over a giant cardboard bingo card waiting to splatter lucky numbers with excrement. There were goldfish in bowls to be won and target shooting ranges, along with "Guess Your Baby's Weight" booths.

The main entertainment was a variety show organized by

Felicia Shaft, the country's most prominent (some would say loudmouthed) pro-lifer and anti-feminist. Marie Osmond was the headliner. The rally also featured the Pro-Life Chorus and several colorful speakers, including Mike Duncannon. The whole event was being taped for the Christian Family Channel, a cable outfit.

Duncannon mingled with the other speakers in the green room while I kept Sherry company down in the first row. She was knitting one of the cute little covers she often made for the jars of fetuses. This one had a big, happy teddy bear right in the middle. She looked very pale and unhappy, but I chalked it up to what had happened between us. We never spoke about the episode afterward, but she did send me a batch of brownies with a note attached that said: "Oops! Weren't we naughty? Hope we can still be friends. Love, Sherry." How do you reply to a batch of brownies after a wonderful night of sex? I decided to try to block out the whole episode.

The lights dimmed and the show began on a spectacular note: over one hundred schoolchildren coming down the aisles holding jars containing fetuses, backlit so that they glowed in the dark, accompanied by the Pro-Life Chorus singing "You Coulda Been a Beautiful Baby." Later Marie sang that weird song about how Billy Joe McAllister jumped off the Tallahatchie Bridge.

Mike Duncannon was next. He came on to great fanfare, with banjos playing "When Irish Eyes Are Smilin." Our office had prepared a great slide presentation for him, and I was anxious to see how it would play. First he showed pictures of himself and Sherry visiting maternity wards and posing with ultrasounds of happy fetuses. (*Brilliant!* I had thought when one of the popsies suggested it. Let's take kissing babies one step further!) But then his speech took on a somber note. He showed slides of Japanese shrines to fetuses and railed on about the high abortion rate in Japan. "And we buy their cars, ladies and gentlemen. We buy their TVs. I ask you, is this what we want to support—the killing of innocent children? The tyranny of so-called free trade?"

Sherry bolted upright, shot out of her seat, and ran up the aisle. I ran after her, not knowing what else to do. Before I knew it, I had followed her into the empty ladies' room, where she barricaded herself in a stall and vomited for what seemed like hours. Fortunately, no one else came in, and I stayed. I didn't want to abandon her.

"Sherry?" I said tentatively.

The toilet flushed and the metal door slowly swung open. Her normally smooth face looked lined and haggard. Big, dark shadows lurked under her eyes.

"Oh, Harry," she said, her head falling onto my chest. "Harry—I'm pregnant."

A whole lot of feelings had flooded through me since Sherry's announcement. How could this happen? I mean, she was a beautiful lady, but certainly not any spring chicken. Was she even young enough to carry a child? And what was she going to do about it? Did she want *me* to do anything about it? I felt paralyzed. I seemed to think of nothing else, and yet I really wasn't thinking about anything. I couldn't get past the initial truth: Sherry was pregnant, and it was my child. The Beltway seed had been sown while I was plowing someone else's field.

I went to work as usual, but nothing seemed the same.

"Earth to Harry," said Day when she was trying to brief me on the delegate count. "You've been mighty distracted. Are you in love, or about to be indicted?"

I heard nothing from Sherry for three days, and then she called me at the office. "Come over to the house tonight, Harry. I'm having a small dinner party."

"Sherry, I—"

"Just come over. Please."

I rode home in the limo with Duncannon and Day, who had also been summoned. Their old parish priest, Father O'Leary, had been invited over. He looked just like Spencer Tracy in *Guess Who's Coming to Dinner.*

"Father!" cried Duncannon. "What brings you here? It's so nice to see you."

"God's work, Mike Duncannon. You're quite the famous one, now, aren't you?"

"Well, Father, what I do is so public—"

"Hang on to your hat, my boy. You are going to be even more famous after tonight."

Sherry flitted around serving drinks and homemade canapés. She looked pretty wonderful. I guess pregnancy had started to agree with her.

We'd consumed three bottles of Chardonnay by the time we sat down to her chicken Kiev dinner. Halfway through, she chose her moment. "Father O'Leary, it was so nice of you to come over. I believe you have something to discuss with all of us."

She had caught the man with a mouthful of poultry. There was a painful silence while we all waited for him to swallow.

"Ah, yes. Sherry has asked me here to confirm and discuss a great miracle. Michael Duncannon, did you know that your wife is with child?"

"Wh-wh-why no," sputtered Duncannon. "But that's impossible. She—I—we—well, you know, we don't *know* each other."

"Yes, yes, I understand that," continued the priest. "Sherry has explained it to me, and on my advice she was even examined by doctors. Mike, I know this is unusual, but I believe we have what might just be the second case of immaculate conception—"

Day snorted and spit out a big piece of chicken. "Hah! Come on, Father. Get real." She began to get up from the table.

"Day, show some respect," said Duncannon.

"Oh, cut the shit, Mike. Show some sense. It's fine with me if you want to be an officially sanctioned cuckold, but count me out. I knew there was a reason I left this lousy church." She started to leave. "Sherry, have a nice baby. You'll be a great mom. But Mike, remember this: You'll *never* be president, even if your wife does give birth to the Messiah!"

She was gone in a flash. Sherry smiled, and I tried to smile back.

Mike turned to me. "So what does this do to our campaign, Harry?"

The next week was tough. We lost Illinois, Michigan, Ohio, and Wisconsin. "I *know* our numbers would have gone up if we had only told them about the news of our Blessed Event," said Duncannon.

"We agreed, sir, that we would wait on that," I reminded him, all the while thinking, *Please God, don't let us be humiliated!*

We were goners, but Duncannon was still acting as if he had the nomination sewn up. He talked confidently about his chances in California, even though we were nine hundred delegates short of the nomination, and Bill Pineapple had already declared himself the nominee. While Duncannon hinted at forming a third party, the perms were having a field day writing his obituary. The op-ed writers were smirking all across America. But it was nothing compared to what they would be saying after the story about Sherry's holy pregnancy would break, and I was sure it would. All I could do was watch and wait.

Office morale was disintegrating. Late in the night, after the scene with Father O'Leary, Day cleaned out her desk and disappeared. Peggy, too, was nowhere to be found and wouldn't return my calls. In my paranoia I imagined she knew that I was the father of Sherry's unborn baby.

The story of the Second Coming was leaking out gradually as Duncannon took more people into his confidence. He was a proud cuckold, I've got to give him that. (I guess if anyone is going to "do" your wife, it might as well be God.)

In the end, it was Barry Orenstein who finally squealed to the press. He even began to talk to the Pineapple campaign right from our offices, within earshot of the whole staff.

I confronted him.

"Well, what do you want me to do?" he asked. "I know you're the son of a preacher man—"

"Grandson," I corrected.

"—but tell me, do you believe this crap? Now I feel like I'm really a laughingstock. Do you know how much flak I've gotten for being a Jew working for Duncannon? But I believed in a lot of his political goals. I was hired to give this campaign credibility. Instead, I end up being medium to Dick Nixon's ghost and midwife to the Antichrist. I've had it, Harry. You'll be hearing from me in the papers. I'm defecting to the Pineapple plantation."

"Me too," said Horace, throwing an arm around his friend. "Power to the Pineapple!"

Later that evening, as I walked out of the office, Barry called me over to the parking lot, where he was standing next to his Saturn station wagon.

"Horace and I talked, and there's something we think we should tell you. You know, he and Peggy and I go way back."

Yes, I did know that. Peggy had told me the whole story of how they had been liberal students together in the late seventies and had slowly gravitated to the Right, how they had discovered that they were a wonderful team on campaigns. The Mod Squad.

"Well," continued Barry. "I know you really love Peggy. She's told me how she feels about you. It's just that—I think this is why she's hiding from you—well, Peggy is not really Peggy. Well, I guess she is, but there is something you should know."

"Yes?" I said.

"Oh, hell," said Barry. "I don't know how to tell you. Did you ever see that movie *The Crying Game*?"

As it turned out, I hadn't. I had been out of the country when the film made its big splash, so I didn't even know what it was about. I rented *The Crying Game* that night. Sure, it was a riveting story about political struggles in Ireland, but I was more interested in the sex. When Stephen Rea fell for that beautiful woman, Jaye Davidson, who turned out to be a man, I just broke down and cried.

Now it all made sense. No wonder my beautiful Peggy never asked for any sexual favors in return. She—or he—was scared of rejection.

I called Peggy right as the credits were rolling. Her answering machine picked up. "Please, darling, I know all about it," I said after the beep. "I have secrets, too. So what? I love you. We'll work it out. Please come back. Nothing is fun without you—and I miss the tofu."

I called her again from California, where we were taking another drubbing in the polls. Still no answer. I left a message saying I would be home the next day. Duncannon seemed more cheerful than ever after our loss in California. A small group of supporters met him outside the hotel, chanting, "San Diego! San Diego! To the Convention, Mike!"

"Thank you, folks," he said. "A lot of people say this fight is over, but we'll fight for what we believe in. We'll go to that convention and we'll storm the doors. We'll fight until the North Pole thaws, and then we'll swim with the sharks all the way home!"

The crowd cheered.

"And, when I'm president, there won't be a place called San Diego. It'll be called something easy to say, something American—like Saint Doug."

The crowd clapped, but only politely. They seemed confused.

"I know we lost today, but what do you expect with all those illegal aliens voting against us?" He stopped, waiting for the applause. None came.

He was slipping, I could tell. We were lucky that not a single perm had shown up to see us leave the hotel. I got him out of there as fast as possible and to the airport, where we boarded a commercial flight home (we had given up our campaign plane six weeks ago). He was acting like a little kid, asking to go see the pilot before we took off. One of the flight attendants, a lovely Baptist woman from Georgia and a Duncannon supporter, was thrilled to bring him into the cockpit for a visit.

I had just thrown my garment bag into the overhead bin and was settling into my seat when I heard an all-too-familiar voice come over the captain's loudspeaker.

"Hello. This is Mike Duncannon, and I'm running for president. I'm pleased that I will be traveling with you across this great country of ours. We'll be flying on a 747, one of the proud descendants of the earliest manpowered flying machines invented here in America by two white men, Orville and Wilbur Wright. Let me remind you, ladies and gentlemen, that Africans didn't invent airplanes. The Japanese—sure, they flew kites, but they woulda never gotten themselves off the ground if it weren't for good old American ingenuity. . . ."

There was the sound of a scuffle and then the speaker system went silent. Duncannon was escorted back by two flight attendants I hadn't noticed earlier, two big black guys who suggested rather firmly that he sit down and get ready for take-off. I had hoped to at least get a little shut-eye on the way back, but the movie on the flight was Oliver Stone's *Nixon,* and Duncannon wouldn't shut up about the inaccuracies. "Look at that, look at that," he said. "Dick would never wear a tie that color. I hope he hasn't seen this."

While we were away, the mice were at play—or, as the case turned out to be, the ratfinks. Barry Orenstein had presented the whole story of Mike Duncannon's mental breakdown—the Nixon sightings, Sherry's Immaculate Conception—to the Pineapple campaign on a silver platter. It was broken to the perms in a big way, with a press conference highlighting Barry's defection from our campaign and his reasons for thinking that Mike was beginning to operate on a delusional plane close to Adolf Hitler's. (The Pineapple press kit cited a speech Mike had made in 1983 calling Hitler "a hard-working guy who was just trying to do his job.")

I called Sherry right after we got back from California. I wanted to tie up loose ends, and I worried that our one night of passion would come back to haunt me.

I needn't have worried. Sherry was starting to *sound* like the Virgin Mary. She seemed to have convinced herself that it was really true. In her mind she had replaced my body and personality with the Holy Ghost. And, ever since the general public had learned her secret, she was reveling in all the attention. In one week she had been on "Regis and Kathie Lee," "The Oprah Winfrey Show," and "A Current Affair." Duncannon encouraged all these appearances, further proof that he had lost his mind. What red-blooded American male would want to admit that he'd never had sex with his wife?

"You're never going to believe it, Harry, but His Holiness called," Sherry was saying. "They're looking into it at the Vatican. Mike and I are flying there in a couple of weeks to talk to him about it." If I hadn't actually seen how much the pope loved Mike Duncannon, I never would have believed it.

I went into the office sporadically, trying to figure out my next step. I spent most of my time fielding strange calls, like the one from an editor at Simon & Schuster who wanted the Duncannons to author a book called *How Not to Do It: Secrets of a Happy Celibate Marriage.* Every day I hoped I would get the nerve to resign, but I couldn't make the break. The campaign had been the only stable part of my life for months. But Mike Duncannon's candidacy was dead, and anyone who had worked for him would probably be tarred forever by his stupid pride in his virginity and his misguided messianic zeal. He was still doing speeches, mostly to audiences of twenty or thirty people at suburban malls. He still spoke of going to the convention in San Diego and raising hell. I don't know. Maybe he and Sherry were planning on going by donkey.

One night the phone rang at my apartment, and I found myself speaking once again to Russ Reeve of the Christian Coalition.

"Trouble in River City, eh, Harry? Paul Rogerson and I have been following it. Now, look, I know Mike looks like he's flaming out right now, but this is all part of the strategy. We want to bring him back for the millennium. A third party, a millennial political party, that's our plan. We'll arrange for him and the missus to go somewhere quiet for the next year or two, and we'll start building grassroots support in the meantime.

He's got it, we know. The people love him. Come work for us in the meantime."

"No thanks," I said. "I'm quitting politics for a while."

"This isn't politics, Harry, it's the Lord's work."

"Well, sir, I'm out of that line, too. I'm a homosexual now, it turns out. Did you know?"

A long silence. "No. I didn't. Did Mike Duncannon realize it?"

"No. I barely knew myself. Don't worry, though, I won't tell. But you can see why my days of service are over."

"Yes. But don't give up, son. Once a Beltway, always a Beltway. You will recover. I have faith."

"Perhaps. I really don't care. It's the most peculiar feeling. Even though I'm a homosexual, I feel confident that someday a son of mine will climb that stairway to heaven."

"Yes," came the terse reply. "Good-bye, Harry. Pray to Jesus. Don't do anything foolish."

I was nearly going out of my mind over Peggy when Horace called.

"Tomorrow night at eight o'clock. The bar at Red Sage. She thinks she's just meeting me and my wife."

"I don't know, Horace. What if she runs away?"

"She won't. Believe me."

"Horace, I gotta know. Who was she before?"

"The same person. But if you're asking about gender, it was the other one. His name was Peter Lindhart, and he made a pretty cool guy. One of my best buddies. But she's a beautiful girl, too, isn't she?"

"Yeah. I'm all confused, Horace. This is virgin territory for me. You think we're going to make it?"

"Not to worry, kid. She's crazy about you. This might even give her that extra push she needs to get the operation."

I met Day Duncannon for lunch the next day. She was leaving for Australia in a week.

"I'm not coming back this time," she said. "By some miracle, I found my true love right here, and we're going to get the hell out of this crazy country. I don't know if it's legal Down Under, Harry, but Brandy Gecko and I are getting married as soon as we get there. Maybe we'll even stop off on the way and do it in Hawaii." She paused to savor my complete surprise.

"Yeah. I know, it's weird," she continued. "I never knew I could swing the other way, either. But she is just the neatest person I've ever met. My kids love her. And she's great in bed, too. Harry, I think you and I are kindred spirits. I heard that something kinda new and different popped up in your love life, too."

I nodded. "Peggy—I mean Peter. Well, I don't know exactly who I mean—yet. Love is a funny thing, Day. I'll never figure it out."

" 'Love has pitched his mansion in the place of excrement.' Yeats. Ever notice how Mike never used that one in any of his speeches?"

"I take it none of the Duncannons will be attending your wedding?"

"Who cares? They didn't come to my last one, just because the bridegroom was Mormon. At weddings the Duncannons always end up puking on the carpet and beating up people in the parking lot anyway. Take care, Harry Beltway. Come down and eat some kangaroo tail soup with us sometime."

Getting back together with Peggy was easier than anything I've ever done. I took one look at her sitting at the bar and ran into her outstretched arms. We didn't even stay for drinks— turns out she had extra tofu hanging around in her fridge.

"You're the only good thing that's ever come out of politics for me," she told me that night.

"Well, I'm a convert," I said, gasping for breath after our first steamy bout of totally consensual sex. "Let's quit this whole scene. Do you think we could buy Soldier Boy's video store and live happily ever after?"

I've never been in love before, and each day I wake up worrying if the feeling will last. But here I am, unemployed and sexually aberrant, and happier than I've ever been.

Channel-surfing the news programs one night, we came upon the Duncannons at the airport, leaving for Italy. "The experts at the Vatican want to compare our unborn baby's DNA with samples from the Shroud of Turin," explained a very serious Mike Duncannon.

"Mr. Duncannon, we hear that you're already organizing a campaign for the year 2000."

Duncannon chuckled. "Yeah. Mike for the Millennium, that's what they're saying. But we'll have to see—that is, if my future son will approve, too."

As I watched Mr. Mike posturing in his old, familiar way for the cameras, I got a kick out of knowing that he was not really talking about his own son. He wasn't even gabbing about God's progeny. Nope, the bun in his wife's oven was mine—Billy Beltway's great-grandson, a kid with messianic blood if there ever was one. I don't know if I can live with the secret forever. Someday, I like to think, I will tell Peggy, and she'll understand. Maybe she'll even laugh.

Peggy and I heard from Mike Duncannon one more time a few weeks later. We were making love when his voice drifted over her phone machine, asking if he and Dick Nixon could come by and bring over a pizza.